10633780

CALGARY PUBLIC LIBRARY

NOV   2015

NATIONAL GEOGRAPHIC
KiDS

ANIMAL RECORDS

KATHY FURGANG AND SARAH WASSNER

THE **BIGGEST,** *FASTEST,* GROSSEST, TINIEST, SLOWEST, AND SMELLIEST CREATURES ON THE PLANET

NATIONAL GEOGRAPHIC
WASHINGTON, D.C.

THE BIGGEST, SMALLEST, FASTEST, SLOWEST, LOUDEST, WEIRDEST, AND DEADLIEST CRITTERS ON THE PLANET

FLIP THE PAGE AND DIVE ON IN!

In *National Geographic Kids' Animal Records* you will learn about the coolest and most curious creatures that have ever run, swam, jumped, flapped, soared, scampered, or slithered their way across planet Earth. Enjoy a front-row seat to see animals go paw-to-claw in species smackdowns, drop in on dinos having a blast from the past, explore the wild world of animal mysteries in the case studies, and test your animal IQ in the fun and games sections. Best of all, you'll read about some awesome researchers and scientists who are going to great lengths to bring it all to you!

Each chapter crowns a king of each category and assigns awards to runners-up, so you'll know all of the weird and wacky ways that winners are determined. You'll read about the largest reptile, the smallest bird, the slowest fish, the cutest killer, the master of disguise, and the most incredible insect. How is it possible that the loudest and deadliest animals on Earth are less than an inch (25 mm) long? Keep reading to find out. There are surprises with every flip of the page!

CHAPTER 1

SAY HELLO TO THE BIGGEST, GRANDEST, MOST GARGANTUAN ANIMALS IN THE WORLD.

These animals are definitely hard to miss, but not all of them boast a big body. While some of them are the tallest, longest, or heaviest for their animal group, others win big for more surprising reasons.

THE **BLUE** WHALE

The blue whale is the largest animal on the planet. Just the tongue of these ocean-dwelling giants can weigh as much as an elephant. And its heart can weigh as much as a car! It takes a lot to feed this 200-ton (181 mt) animal—the blue whale chows down on up to 4 tons (3.6 mt) of krill a day!

TYPE: **MAMMAL**

SCIENTIFIC NAME: **BALAENOPTERA MUSCULUS**

LENGTH: **UP TO 100 FEET (30 M)**

WEIGHT: **UP TO 200 TONS (181 MT)**

DIET: **KRILL**

HABITAT: **OCEANS**

RANGE: **WORLDWIDE**

A BABY BLUE WHALE CAN WEIGH AS MUCH AS **3 TONS** (2.7 MT) AND STRETCH UP TO **25 FEET** (7.6 M) AT BIRTH.

LIFE SPAN: **ABOUT 90 YEARS**

STATUS: **ENDANGERED**

These record holders are huge in their own way. Check out how they top the charts.

BIGGEST LIVING LAND ANIMAL

AFRICAN ELEPHANT

Though it's true that all elephants are big, the African elephant takes the titanic title over its Asian elephant cousin by a few thousand pounds. African elephants can weigh more than 7 tons (6.4 mt), or roughly the same as two safari trucks. On all four feet, the African elephant can stand a whopping 13 feet (4 m) tall at the shoulder.

BIGGEST
INVERTEBRATE (LAND)
COCONUT CRAB

The coconut crab has a leg span of up to 3.3 feet (1 m) and weighs about 6.5 pounds (3 kg). Its name is a perfect fit, too. This tough crustacean is known for punching holes in coconuts!

BIGGEST
INVERTEBRATE (WATER)
COLOSSAL SQUID

This rarely seen deep-sea giant can reportedly reach a mass of more than 1,000 pounds (454 kg) and a length of more than 30 feet (9 m)—not quite as long as its cousin the giant squid (which can grow to more than 40 feet, or 12 m), but still the winner for overall massiveness.

BIGGEST ANIMAL
POPULATION (LAND)
ANTS

The number of ants on Earth is ten billion *billion*. Compare that with the mere seven billion humans on Earth and you can see that we are *very* outnumbered! More than 10,000 known species of ants can be found around the world.

MORE RUNNERS-UP ...

Explore a few more honorable mentions in the colossal creatures category!

BIGGEST CAT
SIBERIAN TIGER

Here, kitty, kitty. Or maybe not! This wild cat can weigh 660 pounds (300 kg) and grow to be 10.75 feet (3.3 m) long. These meat-eaters are known for their power and strength—*purr*fect reason to keep your distance!

BIGGEST REPTILE
SALTWATER CROCODILE

This ferocious crocodile is nicknamed "saltie" because of its great skill as an ocean-water swimmer. It can grow up to 23 feet (7 m) long and weigh more than a ton (0.9 mt). The super-aggressive reptile is big enough to take down a full-grown water buffalo!

14

BIGGEST INSECT

GIANT WETA

Does an insect large enough to eat a full-size carrot send shivers down your spine? Then you might want to shield your eyes from the giant weta—the world's largest creepy-crawly. This hefty 2.5-ounce (71 g) insect looks like a cricket and weighs about as much as three mice.

BIGGEST SPIDER

GOLIATH BIRD-EATING TARANTULA

If you're scared of spiders, don't look now—because here's the largest species. The goliath bird-eating tarantula measures up to a foot (0.3 m) in length, has 1-inch-long (2.5 cm) fangs, and is big enough to eat a bird! If that wasn't bad enough, it even makes a scary hissing noise by rubbing its legs together.

MYSTERY OF THE
MONSTER
FISH

When the enormous carcass of a spiny sea animal washed ashore in Folly Beach, South Carolina, U.S.A., people had to do a double take. The big brown-and-green blob looked just like a prehistoric sea monster! Turns out the creature was actually an Atlantic sturgeon, which can grow up to 15 feet long (4.6 m) and weigh as much as 800 pounds (362.9 kg)! These endangered fish are among the oldest in the world and have tough skin lined with bony spikes, called scutes. It's no wonder they're often called "Dinosaurs of the Sea."

SPECIES: WHALE SHARK

SIZE: UP TO 40 FEET LONG (12.2 M) AND 41,000 POUNDS (18,600 KG)

FISH FACT/FAST FACT:
With a top speed of 3 miles an hour (4.8 km/h), these gentle giants make excellent swim buddies for divers and snorkelers and are the largest fish in the world!

GIANT FISH

Meet three more monsters of the deep!

SPECIES: GIANT OARFISH

SIZE: UP TO 56 FEET (17 M) AND 600 POUNDS (272.2 KG)

FISH FACT/FAST FACT: Deep-sea dwellers, oarfish are rarely seen at the surface. Some believe that if one washes up onshore, it may signal a forthcoming earthquake.

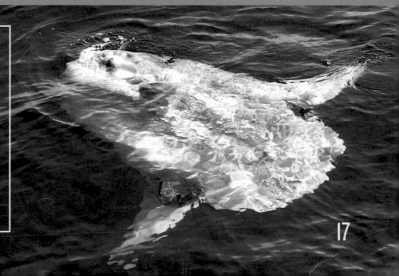

SPECIES: MOLA

SIZE: UP TO 11 FEET (3.4 M) AND 5,000 LBS (2,268 KG)

FISH FACT/FAST FACT: Also known as sunfish, mola are the world's largest bony fish. They get their name because they bask in the sun near the surface of the water.

BIRDS OF A FEATHER

Meet some of the tallest, heaviest, and most fascinating feathered fliers to soar into the record book.

TALLEST FLYING BIRD

SARUS CRANE

Sure. You see plenty of humans who are 6 feet (1.8 m) tall ... but a bird? The sarus crane claims this bragging right, making it the tallest flying bird in the world.

LONGEST BILL

AUSTRALIAN PELICAN

Built-in utensils? What bird wouldn't want a spear attached to its face? The Australian pelican has an 18-inch (46 cm) bill—the longest of any existing bird—that makes grabbing dinner a breeze.

LARGEST **WINGSPAN**

WANDERING ALBATROSS

The wandering albatross's 11.5-foot (3.5 m) wingspan (the distance from one wingtip to the other) is the longest you'll see on any living bird. It's so big that it could probably wrap you and five of your friends in one big bird hug!

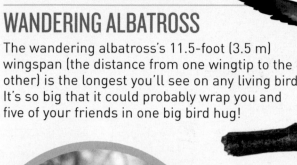

HEAVIEST **FLYING BIRD**

GREAT BUSTARD

This record breaker was dangerously close to extinction because of overhunting. But now the world's heaviest flying bird—one reportedly reached about 46 pounds (21 kg)—is slowly making a comeback, so watch out for this winged heavyweight!

LARGEST **FIELD OF VISION**

WOODCOCK

There's no hiding from this bird—it pretty much sees everything! The woodcock has a 360-degree field of vision, meaning it can see in all directions. The set-back placement of its eyes is the key to this bird's superior stare.

LARGEST **NEST**

BALD EAGLE

When it comes to nests, think of the bald eagles' as megamansions in the sky. Their record-breaking roosts have measured up to 9.5 feet (2.9 m) wide and 20 feet (6 m) high and have weighed more than two tons (1.8 mt).

19

CHART-TOPPING BODY PARTS

My, what *big* eyes you have ... and ears and brains and necks, etc. Check out the cool features that land these creatures in chapter I.

LONGEST **NECK**

GIRAFFE

The tallest living mammal also has the world's longest neck. A giraffe's 8-foot (2.4 m) neck is taller than an adult human! That helps the male giraffe's 18-foot (5.5 m) body tower over other members of the animal kingdom.

LONGEST REPTILE **TONGUE** FOR BODY

CHAMELEON

A chameleon's tongue isn't the longest in the world, but it is longest in proportion to its body. In other words, this reptile's tongue is one-and-a-half times the length of its body. That would be like you having an 8-foot (2.4 m) tongue! Now open wide and say *aahhh!*

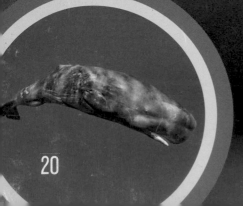

BIGGEST **BRAIN**

SPERM WHALE

About as heavy as two gallons (7.6 L) of milk, the sperm whale's brain weighs in at an average 17 pounds (7.7 kg)! The space it occupies is about 8,000 cubic centimeters, compared with the 1,300 cubic centimeters of a human brain. *Hmm ...* think a sperm whale can help you with your homework?

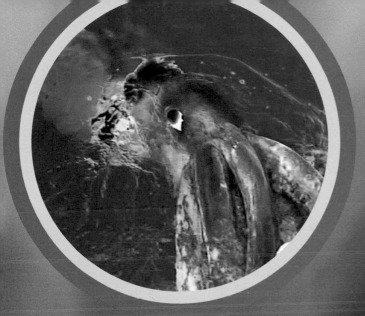

BIGGEST **EYE**
COLOSSAL SQUID

With eyes bigger than dinner plates, the colossal squid has set its sights on breaking records (also check out page 13!). Each of its eyes measures about 11 inches (28 cm) across, and the lenses that let light in are as big as oranges.

LONGEST **HORNS**
WILD WATER BUFFALO

The spread from one tip of the wild water buffalo's horn to the other is about 3.3 feet (1 m) long. Impressive, but it's not all fun and games. Horns this size actually make turning around a challenge for this member of the ox family.

BIGGEST **EARS**
FOR BODY
LONG-EARED JERBOA

Take a look at this little big-eared guy! The jerboa's ears are a third longer than its head and can be about 50 percent the length of its body. That gives it the title of biggest ears in relation to its size, even beating out the rascally rabbit!

THE AMAZING JAPANESE GIANT SALAMANDER

They're slimy, they're smelly, and guess what—they're super-size! Japanese giant salamanders look a lot like the critters you may find in your backyard, but at around 5 feet (1.5 m) and 55 pounds (25 kg), they are actually around ten times longer and 2,000 times heavier than the average salamander. Native to the cold water streams and rivers of northern and western Japan, these amphibians are covered in a thick slime, which keeps them protected from parasites. And if that's not enough to make you steer clear, you may want to avoid backing this giant into a corner. When they're threatened, Japanese giant salamanders secrete a sticky substance that smells like pepper. Well, that's one way to keep your enemies away.

GIANT SALAMANDERS HAVE TEETH ON THE ROOFS OF THEIR MOUTHS.

GIANT SALAMANDERS CAN GO WEEKS WITHOUT EATING.

BATTLE OF THE BRAINS

When it comes to smarts, only one in each pair goes to the head of the class.

WINNER

DOLPHIN vs. WALRUS

Big-brained dolphins are among the most intelligent species on the planet. They outwit all other swimmers in the sea, including the surprisingly smart walrus, which can be trained to do tricks such as singing on demand.

ELEPHANT vs. HIPPO

Scientists are discovering that the smaller the ratio of brain size to body mass, the smarter the animal. Elephants have brains that are roughly 1/560 of their body weight, while hippos have brains that are 1/2789 their body weight.

WINNER

OCTOPUS vs. JELLYFISH

WINNER

Superintelligent octopuses are known to use tools to snag hard-to-reach food. Jellyfish, however, have no brain and instead rely on a simple nervous system to function.

CHIMPANZEE vs. MOUNTAIN GORILLA

WINNER

Though both great apes boast big brains, the chimps' noodles are larger compared to their body size. Able to solve simple problems, they're widely considered to be the smarty-pants of the animal kingdom.

SQUIRREL vs. RABBIT

WINNER

The fluffy-tailed rodents are the winners, paws down! Squirrels are built brainy—they have an innate ability to recall where they stash their nuts. Rabbits rely more on instinct than intellect.

THE GREAT
WEIGH-IN!

29
AFRICAN
ELEPHANTS

=

51
WHITE
RHINOS

=

182
HORSES

=

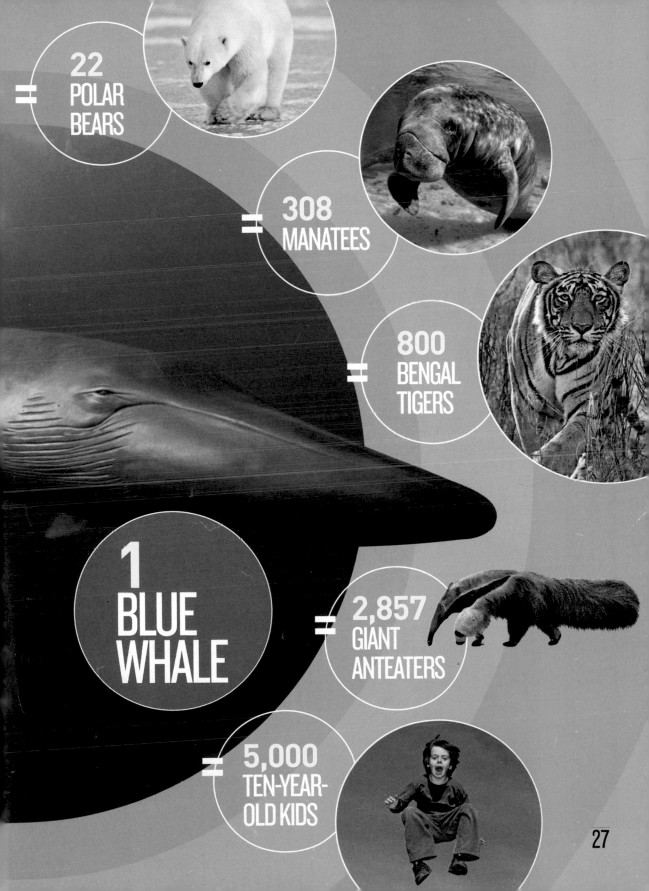

= 22 POLAR BEARS

= 308 MANATEES

= 800 BENGAL TIGERS

1 BLUE WHALE

= 2,857 GIANT ANTEATERS

= 5,000 TEN-YEAR-OLD KIDS

HISTORY'S MOST HULKING DINO

ARGENTINOSAURUS

LIVED DURING: CRETACEOUS PERIOD (94 MILLION YEARS AGO)

LOCATION: ARGENTINA

HEIGHT: UP TO 26 FEET (8 M)

WEIGHT: UP TO 77 TONS (70 MT)

LENGTH: UP TO 115 FEET (35 M)

One of the biggest dinosaurs to ever roam the Earth was the *Argentinosaurus*. Reaching a height of 26 feet (8 m) and weighing roughly 77 tons (70 mt), this large lizard was as long as a jumbo jet and towered higher than a two-story building. But for a creature that weighed more than 800 modern-day adult humans, it certainly started out itty-bitty. At birth, *Argentinosaurus* weighed only about 11 pounds (5 kg)—not even twice as much as a human baby. To reach such epic proportions, this dino chowed down on enough plants each day to take in the same amount of calories as in 50 chocolate cakes! But there's a downside to that kind of growth spurt—each prehistoric poop equaled about 32 pints (15 L). Yuck!

BIG-AT-A-GLANCE

FROGHOPPER

COMMON SHREW

1 BIGGEST INSECT JUMPER

This 0.2-inch (0.5 cm) bug jumps up to 28 inches (71 cm) high. If humans jumped this same distance relative to body size, we could easily soar over a 690-foot (210 m) skyscraper!

2 BIGGEST NONSTOP MIGRATION

In 2007, one of these fearless fliers migrated from Alaska to New Zealand without stopping for food or drink. The 7,145-mile (11,500 km) trip took nine days.

3 BIGGEST EATER

This little creature really enjoys pigging out! It eats up to 90 percent of its body weight every day. Think you'd want to trade places? Think again. This shrew feasts mostly on a bug buffet, but it also enjoys delicious worms, snails, and slugs.

4 BIGGEST NUMBER OF BIRTHDAYS

The ocean quahog takes the cake for the most number of birthdays. These sea creatures have been known to live more than 400 years. That's a lot of candles!

BAR-TAILED GODWIT

OCEAN QUAHOG

RHINOCEROS
BEETLE

THE MUSCLE POWER OF THE MIGHTY BEETLE

Imagine you could lift 850 times your own body weight, just like the rhinoceros beetle. For a grown human to pull off this kind of stunt, he or she would have to lift almost 80 tons (72.6 mt)—or a stack of about 40 cars. Don't try this at home!

5 BIGGEST WEIGHT LIFTER

Step aside, human weaklings! Ounce for ounce, the rhinoceros beetle is considered the world's strongest creature. It may be tiny, but it can lift 850 times its own body weight.

6 BIGGEST EGG

The largest living bird also lays the world's largest eggs! Ostriches can produce eggs more than 6 inches (15 cm) long and that weigh more than 3 pounds (1.4 kg). But this is actually small considering the size of the mother: Females can weigh more than 240 lbs (109 kg) and achieve a height of 6 feet (1.8 m).

7 BIGGEST HABITAT

Wherever you are on Earth, krill aren't too far away! This tiny ocean creature is abundant in all of the world's oceans, which cover about 70 percent of our planet. You can find them swimming around everywhere, even miles under the sea.

8 LONGEST WORM

An average bootlace worm is up to 50 feet (15 m) long, but that's nothing compared with the longest of these writhing wigglers. The largest bootlace worm ever discovered measured in at 180 feet (55 m)!

OSTRICH EGG

KRILL

BOOTLACE WORM

OCTOPUSES: BIG BRAINS AND BIG SMARTS

So you read on page 25 that octopuses are supersmart, but did you know that scientists study their brains to learn more about yours? Proportionate to size, octopuses have the largest and most complex brains of all invertebrates. Their brains are very different from ours, yet octopuses display some of the same smarts: They recognize their own names, solve puzzles, and pry open childproof jars.

By studying octopus brains, researchers think they can learn about how our own noggins store and recall information. They also hope to figure out how the eight-armed eggheads display humanlike actions while having such a unique nervous system. And perhaps they might even discover ways that human intelligence could evolve.

OCTOPUSES HAVE THREE HEARTS.

AN OCTOPUS BRAIN HAS ABOUT 300 MILLION NEURONS (NERVE CELLS).

NAME THOSE TEETH!

All of these animals are known for their giant chompers. Can you match the teeth with the correct species?

A

1

2

B

ANSWERS
1:C; 2:D;
3:E; 4:B; 5:A

34

AND THE WINNER IS ...

SCIENTIFIC NAME:
**PHYLUM
TARDIGRADA**

TYPE: **INVERTEBRATE**

LENGTH: **0.004-0.02
INCHES (0.1- 0.5 MM)**

HABITAT: **MARINE, FRESHWATER,
AND DAMP LAND ENVIRONMENTS**

DIET: **ALGAE, FUNGI, BACTERIA, PLANT MATTER**

TARDIGRADE [WATER BEAR]

RANGE: WORLDWIDE

LIFE SPAN: FROM 3 TO 30 MONTHS

The world's smallest visible animal is smaller than a poppy seed, yet it's one tough cookie. The tardigrade is an eight-legged wonder that generally hangs out in water or damp places, from great depths to heights reaching thousands of feet. This amazing aquatic creature can also survive in just about any extreme condition you can think of. Boiling water, ice cold, radiation, and even the pressure of space are no problem for this tiny toughie. Its minuscule body responds by drying out and going into a kind of hibernation. Some species can do this for a decade or longer! When conditions return to normal, so can they.

THE RUNNERS-UP ...

These record setters are the tiniest in their categories. But despite their small size, these animals boast some truly incredible features.

SMALLEST
BIRD

BEE HUMMINGBIRD

This tiny bird can grow to be only about 2.4 inches (6 cm) long and weighs a mere 0.07 ounces (1.9 g). Half of its body length is made up of its bill and tail. But what's really amazing about this wonder is that it can hover in midair and drink up to eight times its body mass in water daily!

SMALLEST
AMPHIBIAN
TINY FROG

This 0.3-inch (7.7 mm) frog can fit on a dime and jump 30 times longer than its body size! Scientists have recently found this and other tiny frog species living among leaf litter on the floor of Papua New Guinea's rain forest. They were led to the amazing amphibians by listening to their mini-frog calls and zeroing in on the source of the high-pitched sounds.

SMALLEST **DOG**
CHIHUAHUA

Chihuahuas are the winners here in more ways than one! The record holders for smallest dog are two of the most compact canines around. Heaven Sent Brandy takes the title for shortest length, at just 6 inches (15.2 cm) from her nose to the tip of her tail. And Miracle Milly's the tiniest in terms of height, standing just 3.8 inches (9.65 cm) tall.

BRANDY

MILLY

SMALLEST
KANGAROO
MUSKY RAT-KANGAROO

A 17.6-ounce (500 g) kangaroo? These insect-eating animals live in the Australian rain forest and sleep in nests made of material they gather with their own tail.

Here are four more tiny critters that break some pretty big records.

SMALLEST OCTOPUS

OCTOPUS WOLFI

There are some 300 species of octopuses in the world, but this tiny one blows them all out of the water. It's just 0.6 inches (1.5 cm), weighs less than 0.04 ounces (1 g), and can fit right on the tip of your nose.

SMALLEST FISH

PAEDOCYPRIS PROGENETICA

In the forest swamps of Sumatra, you might easily overlook this tiny fish from the carp family. After all, it's only one-third of an inch (7.9 mm) long and one of the smallest vertebrates. Making it tougher to spot: The fish's body is see-through!

SMALLEST
MAMMAL
KITTI'S HOG-NOSED BAT

This cave-dwelling creature is not only the tiniest bat but also the smallest mammal alive. Sometimes called the "bumble-bee bat," it weighs less than 0.07 ounces (2 g) and reaches lengths of up to only 1.3 inches (3.3 cm)—about the size of a large bumblebee!

SMALLEST **CHAMELEON**
BROOKESIA MICRA

Among the smallest reptiles in the world is the tiny *Brookesia micra* chameleon. At barely more than an inch (28.8 mm) maximum in total length, the scaly Madagascar native can perch on the tip of your finger.

43

WORLD'S SMALLEST PET PIG!

In many ways, Huckleberry Finn is a lot like the average pig: He likes to munch on grass, play in the mud, and squeal when he's happy. But this pint-size pig is truly one of a kind. Not only does he live with his owner in a San Francisco, California, U.S.A., apartment, but he's also considered to be the world's smallest pet pig! A Juliana pig (also known as a teacup pig because of its small size), "H-Finn" was only about the size of an iPad Mini at birth. Now, he weighs as much as a newborn baby and can fit into a shoe box. The precious little piggy likes to take long walks on a leash around the city and sleeps in a little house with blankets. He even sits on command and uses a litter box. Now that's one smart swine!

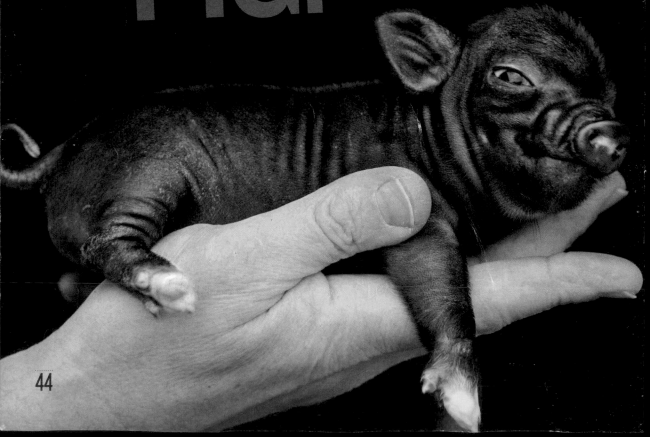

LUCY THE DOG

Weighing less than a small chicken, this Yorkie is a therapy dog who spends time visiting patients and children's hospitals. She holds the record for the world's smallest working dog.

MORE MINI-PETS!

PIP THE HEDGEHOG

This prickly critter is so tiny, he can comfortably fit into a coffee cup! But he doesn't need any java to stay awake—pygmy hedgehogs are nocturnal animals and are known to run on hamster wheels all night long!

EINSTEIN THE HORSE

This domesticated horse stands only 20 inches (50.8 cm) tall and weighs 85 pounds (38.5 kg). He runs around the house, eats from a bowl, and snuggles on the couch with his owners.

Sure, most things have to be seen to be believed, but when it comes to microscopic creatures, you'll have to trust the experts! Take a look at the pictures below for your own glimpse into their teeny-tiny world.

MICROSCOPIC WONDERS

ROTIFERS

Rotifers have multiple body parts and hundreds of cells. Why is that amazing? Because most of phylum Rotifera's more than 2,000 species are less than 0.04 inches (1 mm) long (although some can reach up to 0.1 inch, or 3 mm)! Rotifers mostly live in freshwater environments such as lakes, ponds, streams, and even puddles.

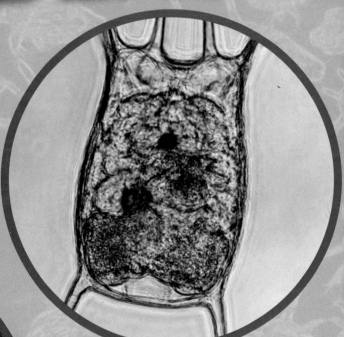

DUST MITES

It's a good thing you can't see these creepy-crawlies without a microscope. At only 0.008 to 0.012 inches (0.2–0.3 mm) long, these animals are everywhere. About 100,000 to 2 million of them can live on one mattress! And if that's not weird enough ... they feast on your dead skin!

NEMATODES

These wormlike organisms (also known as roundworms) are an important part of our soil and mud, partly because they are so nutrient rich. Members of phylum Nematoda can be found in nearly every habitat on Earth! The smallest species of nematodes are microscopic, but some can grow large enough to be spotted by human eyes.

COPEPODS

The average length of an adult in these diverse species of aquatic crustaceans is about 0.04 to 0.08 inches (1–2 mm). They live in water in a variety of habitats all over Earth, including caves, mountains, and ocean trenches. Their name comes from the Greek words meaning "oar" and "foot" because their swimming legs look like oars.

CLADOCERANS

Also known as a water flea, the cladoceran is a tiny crustacean that mostly lives in fresh-water habitats such as lakes, ponds, streams, and rivers. Most don't get much longer than 0.24 inches (6 mm). Even though it's in the same animal group as the lobster, this peewee water lover gets around virtually unnoticed!

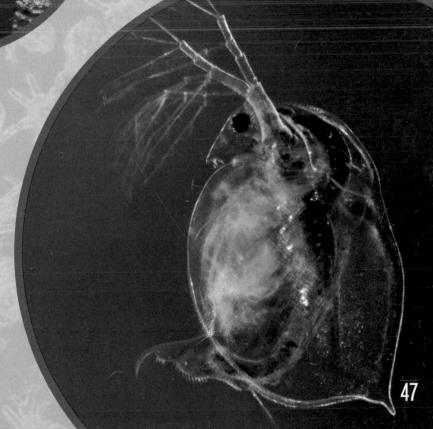

HOME SWEET HOME

The Galápagos Islands make up about 3,000 square miles (7,770 sq km) of land in the Pacific Ocean. Some species of animals on these islands can't be found any place else on Earth. That means they have one of the smallest geographic ranges in the world. Check out these cool creatures that live no other place on the planet!

GALÁPAGOS MARINE IGUANA

This funny-looking reptile is the world's only water-loving lizard. It grazes on algae that it scrapes off the surface of rocks and in shallow waters near shore. Larger ones will even dive into the cold sea for short periods to find some yummy seaweed! The white on its head is salt from the seawater that it sneezes out while cleaning the glands near its nose. *Achoo!*

GALÁPAGOS GIANT TORTOISE

The islands are home to the world's largest and longest-living tortoise, the Galápagos giant tortoise. It can reach 550 pounds (250 kg) and live in the wild for about 100 years. Galápagos is the Spanish word for "tortoise"—early explorers named the islands after this stunning creature.

GALÁPAGOS
LAND SNAIL

As small as about an inch long
(25 mm), these animals are
some of the tiniest endangered creatures endemic to
the Galápagos. Approximately
60 bulimulid snail species are
found throughout the islands,
many having become endan-
gered due to invasive species
and human activity.

GALÁPAGOS **PENGUIN**

This penguin is the only species of its family
found at or just north of the equator and has
the smallest population of any penguin on
Earth. Galápagos penguins live on land, lying
on their bellies on the rocky beach, but they
swim and hunt for food in the water.

FLIGHTLESS **CORMORANT**

Here's a bird that would rather swim than fly.
In fact, the flightless cormorant has lost the
ability to fly! Why? It has no predators and
plenty of food. Over time its wings got smaller
and weaker, while its swimming legs got
stronger. This rare bird is found on only two
of the islands in the Galápagos region.

SMALL BUT DEADLY

Found in the creeks and swamps of coastal New South Wales, Australia, the recently discovered eastern swamp crayfish *(Gramastacus lacus)* reaches a length of only 0.84 inches (21.3 mm) and a weight of just 0.25 ounces (7 g). These creatures might be teeny, but they will not be messed with! They sport large, long chelae (claws) to defend themselves, which they open and wave around rapidly to deter attacks by predators, including other crayfish.

Unfortunately, these small wonders are potentially endangered, suffering habitat loss as a result of coastal development.

LAKE YABBIES (A SPECIES OF CRAYFISH) CAN BURROW UP TO 3 FEET (0.9 M) DEEP, WHICH HELPS THEM SURVIVE LONG DRY SPELLS.

CRAYFISH SWIM BACKWARD WHEN THREATENED.

TINY TERRORS

Bigger doesn't always mean stronger! Check out who would win if these animals faced off in the wild.

NORTHERN SHORT-TAILED SHREW **VS.** GARTER SNAKE

You'd think the tiny, mole-like rodent would be no match for the slithering snake. Think again. With one bite of its powerful jaws, the shrew can actually paralyze its prey with saliva—and eat the snake alive.

WINNER

BLACK RAT **VS.** ORIENTAL RAT FLEA

Rats, beware! One bite from these bacteria-carrying fleas, which feed on the blood of mammals, can lead to a deadly infection and transmit tapeworm larvae along with a host of other diseases.

WINNER

WINNER

REGAL HORNED LIZARD **VS.** BOBCAT

This lizard may seem like an easy catch for the bobcat, but the second the mammal tries to rumble, the reptile shoots blood straight out of its eye. Not only does this tactic distract the cat, but the blood tastes bad, too, causing the furry fiend to back away.

Meat lovers with supersharp teeth and claws, wolverines usually enjoy carrion (dead animal carcasses) or smaller prey such as rodents and rabbits. But they may also attack much bigger animals, like caribou, by hiding in brush or behind a rock and then stealthily pouncing on their unsuspecting prey.

CARIBOU **VS.** WOLVERINE

WINNER

WINNER

Packing a double punch—a deadly bite and razor-sharp jaws—this spider is still no match for bloodsucking jumper ants. The ants' painful sting partially paralyzes prey, so they can feast on much larger insects.

HUNTSMAN SPIDER **VS.** JACK JUMPER ANT

BORN ITTY-BITTY!

Oh, baby! Check out how small these awesome animals are at birth!

KOALA

=

DIME

POLAR BEAR

=

HOT DOG

KANGAROO

=

JELLY BEAN

OPOSSUM = HONEY BEE

 = PEA

BLUE-RINGED OCTOPUS

TWO-TOED SLOTH

 = PLASTIC WATER BOTTLE

PANDA BEAR = STICK OF BUTTER

WINGED MYSTERY

A fossil from this petite predator was first uncovered in 2000 in China. But there was something even cooler about this "new" dino than its size. It had birdlike feathers attached to all four of its limbs. This four-winged dinosaur threw scientists into a tizzy. What were these extra wings used for, they wondered. Did the extra wings make flight more efficient? Faster? Smoother? Or were they used for some other purpose? Many scientists think this tiny beast is the missing link to understanding how today's birds evolved. And who doesn't love a good mystery?

MICRORAPTOR

LIVED DURING: **EARLY CRETACEOUS PERIOD (125 MILLION YEARS AGO)**

LOCATION: **CHINA**

LENGTH: **31.5 INCHES (0.8 M)**

HEIGHT: **11.8 INCHES (0.3 M)**

WEIGHT: **2.2–4.4 POUNDS (1–2 KG)**

A Tie for the Tiniest Dino?

Not so fast, *Microraptor!* The *Parvicursor* challenges you for the title of smallest dinosaur! Its name means "tiny runner," but the little critter looks more like it's ready to dance than run. More fossils need to be found of this bird-beaked, bony-legged runner to see if it's just a baby and if there are larger, adult-size *Parvicursor* fossils lurking in the rocks somewhere.

IVORY-BILLED WOODPECKER

GIRAFFE

SMALL-AT-A-GLANCE

1 SMALLEST POPULATION

There are so few of these birds left that scientists believed the species was already extinct. But a 2005 video shows that the wily woodpecker may still be out there! Sightings in the past decade, however, are uncon-firmed, so the precise number remains unknown.

2 SMALLEST NEST

How would you like a house the size of a penny? That's the size of this bird's nesting area. Some hummingbirds build their nests so that they are shallow like a nutshell, while others build them so they are narrow, like a thimble.

3 SMALLEST SLEEPER

In the wild, the giraffe sleeps about five minutes at a time, about four or six times per day. Add it up and that's only about half an hour of sleep per day! For a human, that would be a serious shortage of shut-eye.

HUMMINGBIRD NEST

SNAIL

SMALLEST PRIMATE

4 In the Amazon rain forest lives a quick, 4.2-ounce (120 g) ball of fur, able to bound 16 feet (5 m) in just one leap. The pygmy marmoset's head and body are just about 5 inches (13 cm) long—but its tail is 8 inches (20 cm) long, making swinging and balancing on branches a breeze!

SMALLEST TEETH

5 Imagine the size of a snail's mouth. Then imagine that mouth filled with thousands of teeth. A cavity-free check up at the dentist would be a challenge for sure!

SMALLEST WINGSPAN

6 From tip to tip, this tiny Tanzanian terror's wings are only 0.01 inches (0.3 mm) long. That's smaller than a grain of sand!

PYGMY MARMOSET

TANZANIAN PARASITIC WASP

COCKROACH CAM

COCKROACHES HAVE BEEN ON EARTH FOR MORE THAN 300 MILLION YEARS.

THERE ARE MORE THAN 4,000 SPECIES OF COCKROACHES IN THE WORLD.

Usually, the only thing cockroaches are good for is giving you the heebie-jeebies. But now, scientists are putting these pests to work. By mounting tiny cameras onto the bugs' backs, researchers at North Carolina State University are hoping they'll be able to steer them into small spaces and buildings undetected—and may even help humans during a disaster. How does it work? First, scientists fit electrodes into the insects' antennas, which allows them to "steer" the roach using a simple remote control. Then, they fit the bugs with tiny backpacks carrying a locator beacon and a mini-microphone that could be used to listen for distress calls.

In the wild, how do the small survive?
By hiding in plain sight!

NOW YOU SEE THEM ...
OR DO YOU?

CAN YOU LOCATE
THE LITTLE CRITTER
CAMOUFLAGED
IN EACH PICTURE?

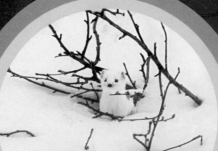

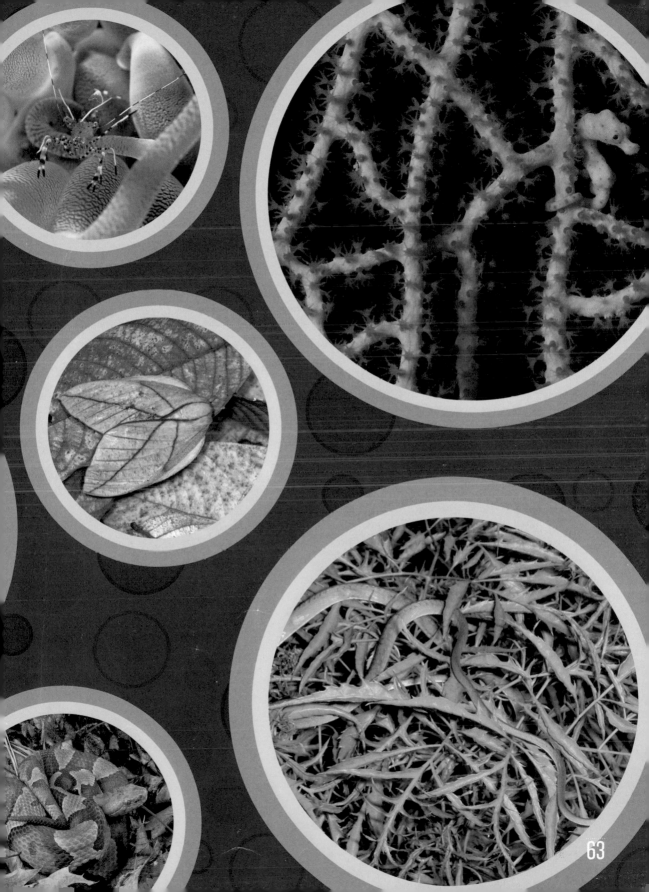

CHAPTER 3

POP QUIZ

WHAT'S COVERED IN FUR, FEATHERS, OR SCALES AND SPEEDIER THAN YOUR BROTHER TRYING TO MAKE IT TO SCHOOL ON TIME?

ANSWER: Many of the animals in this chapter!

The natural world is chock-full of rapid racers, swift swimmers, and fast fliers. And while measuring the momentum of every member of the animal kingdom is nearly impossible, here are some of the creatures known for their need for speed.

PEREGRINE
FALCON

Which fleet flier can swoop down from the sky to catch its prey at up to 200 miles an hour (320 km/h)? The peregrine falcon! Clocking in at number one in the quickness countdown, this bird is not too shabby at horizontal flying speeds, either. It can reach up to 34 miles an hour (55 km/h) when it's just out for a pleasure cruise.

SCIENTIFIC NAME: **FALCO PEREGRINUS**

TYPE: **BIRD**

LENGTH: **UP TO 19.3 INCHES (49 CM); WINGSPAN UP TO 3.6 FEET (1.1 M)**

WEIGHT: **UP TO 56.4 OUNCES (1.6 KG)**

STATUS: **LEAST CONCERN**

DIET: **MAINLY BIRDS**

LIFE SPAN: **UP TO 17 YEARS IN THE WILD**

HABITAT: **DIVERSE; HOT, COLD, DESERTS, FORESTS, WETLANDS, MARITIME ISLANDS, PLAINS, MOUNTAINS**

RANGE: **WORLDWIDE EXCEPT ANTARCTICA**

These swift specimens super-speed past the competition!

FASTEST LAND ANIMAL

CHEETAH

The world's fastest land mammal can go from 0 to 60 miles an hour (96.5 km/h) in just three seconds. First cheetahs scan their surroundings and wait for prey—then *bam!*—they sprint for their target and pounce before the unsuspecting animal knows what hit it.

FASTEST
RUNNING BIRD

OSTRICH

These flightless birds can run more than 31 miles an hour (50 km/h) for long distances. Even more impressive, ostriches can bolt up to 44 miles an hour (70 km/h) for short sprints, covering up to 16 feet (5 m) of ground in a single stride. Now those are some lightning-fast legs!

FASTEST
PRIMATE

PATAS MONKEY

When it comes to outrunning predators, the patas monkey leaves most animals in the dust. This long-limbed primate can reach speeds of 34 miles an hour (55 km/h) in its effort to escape lions, hyenas, and other predatory animals in its African habitats.

FASTEST
SMALL MAMMAL

ELEPHANT SHREW

Also called a sengi, this pointy-snouted creature weighs a little more than a pound (500 g) and runs remarkably well for its small stature. Don't blink or you'll miss this short-legged sprinter, which can reach speeds of more than 17 miles an hour (28 km/h)!

Here are some more animals that spend their lives in the fast lane.

FASTEST SMALL MARINE MAMMAL

DALL'S PORPOISE

Of all small marine mammals—if up to 485 pounds (220 kg) can be called "small"!—the Dall's porpoise wins the blue ribbon for swift swimming: It can propel up to 34 miles an hour (55 km/h) for short distances. And these cool-water cetaceans usually swim with their buddies; groups of up to 200 have been reported riding the waves together!

70

FASTEST **WATER-DIVING BIRD**

GENTOO PENGUIN

No other diving bird can reach the speeds of the gentoo penguin, which tops out at 22 miles an hour (35 km/h) when propelling headfirst into icy waters. That would be impressive for one dive—but this powerful penguin makes the dive up to 450 times a day in search of food!

FASTEST **GROWING CORAL**

STAGHORN CORAL

The fastest growing of all western Atlantic corals, this Caribbean invertebrate's branches grow up to 8 inches (20 cm) a year. The staghorn coral is aptly named because its branches look like—you guessed it—the antlers of a stag (male deer).

FASTEST **FISH**

SAILFISH

Racing like a car on the highway, the sailfish can swim up to 68 miles an hour (109 km/h) in short bursts. This fast fish uses its speed, as well as the giant dorsal fin on its back, to corral schools of sardines and anchovies for dinner.

THE SCIENCE OF SPEED!

Like finely tuned machines, cheetahs are built for precision and power. Check out what makes these big cats so fast.

SPRINGY SPINE
As it runs, a cheetah's spine recoils like a spring, giving it the ability to take extra-long strides that can reach up to 26 feet (8 m).

TOP TAIL
A long tail counter-balances its weight and serves as a rudder, swishing back and forth and keeping the big cat balanced and letting it easily change direction.

MEGAMUSCLES
Cheetah's use their strong hind leg muscles to explode with power with every stride.

LONG LEGS
Thanks to its long limbs, a sprinting cheetah can cover the length of a stretch limousine in one stride!

STEADY HEAD
The small, lightweight head holds steady while running, keeping the cheetah super aerodynamic.

EXTRA AIR
What big nostrils you have! Expanded nasal cavities let the cheetah take in more oxygen.

FAST FEET
Blunt claws and hard foot pads act like built-in soccer cleats, helping it dig into the ground and gain traction.

FAST FEATURES
When it comes to speed, these species are no slouches! Here's what helps to make these creatures quick:

SAILFISH
TOP SPEED: **68 MPH (109 KM/H)**

FAST FEATURES: A long pointed bill and a streamlined body work together to help this fish stealthily slice through the water.

PEREGRINE FALCON
TOP SPEED: **200 MPH (320 KM/H) WHEN DIVING FOR PREY**

FAST FEATURES: Dominant chest muscles lend the bird a boost as it flaps its long, curved wings. Slim and stiff feathers also make for a sleek, aerodynamic physique.

HAWK MOTH
TOP SPEED: **12 MPH (19 KM/H)**

FAST FEATURES: Long narrow forewings and a streamlined abdomen help this bug fly faster than many birds.

SPINY-TAILED IGUANA
TOP SPEED: **21 MPH (34 KM/H)**

FAST FEATURES: Strong hind legs provide power, while a long tail lets this lizard gain speed without falling over.

Whether they skitter, hop, or fly, these creepy-crawlies leave the rest in the dust.

TURBO ARTHROPODS!

FASTEST SWARM

LOCUSTS

When these grasshopper-looking insects move through an area in a swarm, they waste no time. The large group can cover 460 square miles (1,191 sq km) and pack up to 80 million locusts in less than a half square mile (1.3 sq km). A swarm that size could eat 423 million pounds (192 million kg) of plants in just one day.

FASTEST FLIER

AUSTRALIAN DRAGONFLY

Look, up in the sky! It's a bird, it's a plane, it's ... the Australian dragonfly! This speedy insect can reach a speed of 36 miles an hour (58 km/h).

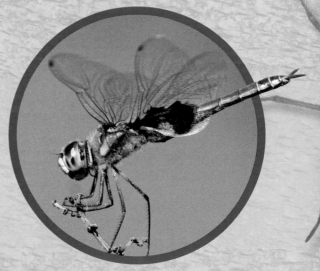

FASTEST WING BEAT

FRUIT FLY

If you got a dollar for every beat of the fruit fly's wings, you'd earn more than $200 every second. Not too shabby!

FASTEST **CRAWLER**

TIGER BEETLE

This speedy crawler can dart away at 5.6 miles an hour (9 km/h). Oddly enough, the insect becomes blind as it runs, so it must use its antennae to guide its way.

FASTEST **BITE**

TRAP-JAW ANT

Did you just blink? This insect can close its mandibles 2,300 times faster than that, snapping its jaws shut at a speed of up to 145 miles an hour (233 km/h)! These amazing ants can also use their remarkable jaw speed to escape potential predators, aiming their chompers at the ground and sending themselves more than 3 inches (7.6 cm) in the air.

FASTEST **SPIDER**

GIANT HOUSE SPIDER

With a body length of only 0.59 inches (1.5 cm), this rapid arachnid can run 1.73 feet a second (0.53 m/s). That's 34 times its own body length covered in a flash. Imagine how fast you could run with eight legs!

FASTEST COSTUME CHANGERS

Camouflage is a handy defense for all crafty creatures—but these quick-change artists do it with impressive speed!

GOLDEN TORTOISE BEETLE

This odd-looking beetle can quickly change from shiny gold to shades of red, orange, or brown (sometimes with spots!). It does this to attract a mate or when pestered by predators.

CHRYSSO SPIDER

Species of this compact crawler have been observed to quickly change color when disturbed. Guess their spider sense must be tingling!

MIMIC OCTOPUS

Keep an eye on this fast-changing animal and you'll see an amazing transformation: a creature able to imitate its surroundings and virtually disappear.

CUTTLEFISH

This animal's nervous system enables it to change "outfits" on command. This allows the cuttlefish to "hypnotize" its prey before going in for the grab with its tentacles.

PEACOCK FLOUNDER

Wonder where that peacock flounder went? It uses one of its eyes to recognize the color and pattern in its ocean-floor environment—and then it blends in!

FLATFISH

You may think you're looking at specks of sand on the ocean floor, but look closer and you'll see the outline of the flatfish lying on the ground. Now that's some insta-camo!

77

MANTIS
MADNESS

A scientist recently discovered not just one but *19* new species of mantises—and they all happen to be super-fast! Known as bark mantises, these bugs, found exclusively in trunks and branches of trees in the Central and South America rain forests, are smaller, flatter, and broader than the commonly known praying mantis. And instead of relying on sneak attacks to capture prey like their bigger cousins do, these insects actually chase their chow. Their speediness also lets them quickly scurry to safety when approached by potential predators such as birds and frogs.

But their speed isn't the only thing that makes these matids cool. To keep track of the many different species, the bugs were given names such as *Liturgusa krattorum* (after the Kratt brothers of *Wild Kratts*) and *Liturgusa algorei* (in honor of former U.S. vice president and environmental activist Al Gore). Some are even named after the young daughters of the scientist who discovered them.

MANTISES CAN TURN THEIR HEADS AROUND 180 DEGREES.

BARK MANTISES PLAY DEAD ON THE FOREST FLOOR TO AVOID BEING EATEN BY PREDATORS.

FAST CLASH

Which animal would win in a race for first place?

WINNER

BOTTLENOSE DOLPHIN **vs.** HUMAN

WHO'S A SPEEDIER SWIMMER?

Although some humans can certainly cut through the water at amazing speeds, the world's best swimmers reach only about 4.5 miles an hour (7.2 km/h). Dolphins, which can swim up to 100 miles (160.9 km) a day, hit up to 19 miles an hour (30.6 km/h).

MALLARD (DUCK) **vs.** HOUSE SPARROW

WHO FLIES FASTER?

Ducks may not seem like the speediest birds, but most waterfowl can fly 40 to 60 miles an hour (64–97 km/h)! Stocky sparrows average speeds of only up to about 30 miles an hour (48.3 km/h).

WINNER

WHO'S A QUICKER CLIMBER?

Geckos climb almost as fast as they run on the ground, covering about 3 feet (1 m) each second. In a race to the top of a wall, the reptile would outrun the spider, which clocks speeds of up to 2 feet (0.6 m) per second.

WINNER

GECKO VS. WOLF SPIDER

JACKRABBIT VS. KANGAROO

WHO'S THE SWIFTER LEAPER?

Hopping on just two feet, kangaroos can really crank up the speed, topping 40 miles an hour (64 km/h) over short distances. Even more impressive, a 2-foot-long (0.6 m) jackrabbit can match that speed when escaping a predator.

TIE

HORSE VS. CAMEL

WHO IS FASTER OVER LONG DISTANCES?

The camel can keep up a swift pace of about 25 miles an hour (40 km/h) for more than 20 miles (32 km). That's like running a marathon in 1 hour, 2 minutes—more than an hour better than the fastest human. Horses maintain only about 10.5 miles an hour (17 km/h) over long distances.

WINNER

SPECIES SPEEDOMETER

How fast can they go?

MOUSE
8 MPH
(13 KM/H)

BLACK MAMBA
12.5 MPH
(20 KM/H)

SLOTH
0.15 MPH
(0.24 KM/H)

GARDEN SNAIL
0.03 MPH
(0.05 KM/H)

SEAHORSE
0.01 MPH
(0.016 KM/H)

HUMAN
28 MPH
(45 KM/H)

GRIZZLY
BEAR
30 MPH
(48 KM/H)

OSTRICH
40 MPH
(64 KM/H)

THOMSON'S
GAZELLE
50 MPH
(80 KM/H)

CHEETAH
70 MPH
(113 KM/H)

DINO SPEED RACER

COMPSOGNATHUS

Scientists designed complicated models and performed elaborate calculations to figure out that *Compsognathus* was the fastest dinosaur to ever run along Earth's surface. It reached top speeds of almost 40 miles an hour (64 km/h). Think of that as somewhere between the speeds of a horse galloping and a cheetah sprinting. This chicken-size creature owed its speed to its hollow bones and strong birdlike legs. Its long tail helped it balance as it reached top sprinting speeds. Speed was a handy quality to have in the late Jurassic period!

LIVED DURING: LATE JURASSIC PERIOD (150 MILLION YEARS AGO)

LOCATION: EUROPE

WEIGHT: 9 POUNDS (4 KG)

HEIGHT: 2.3 FEET (0.7 M)

LENGTH: 2.13 FEET (0.65 M)

FAST-AT-A-GLANCE

PLAINS SPADEFOOT TOAD

MANTIS SHRIMP

1 FASTEST HATCHING TOAD

In the toad world, this creature spends the shortest time in its shell. Eggs often hatch within only 48 hours of being laid.

2 FASTEST ADULTHOOD

Many humans can't do much more in five minutes than scarf down a bowl of ice cream, but a female mayfly species called *Dolania americana* lives its entire adult life in less than five minutes! After a year living in its nymph form at the bottom of a stream, it comes to the surface for a superfast adulthood—it finds a mate, lays eggs, and checks out.

3 FASTEST PUNCH

The claw of this powerful animal whacks its prey like the strike of a hammer—and the power punch happens 50 times faster than you can blink an eye. The mantis shrimp knocks its prey out immediately and will often shatter the shells of the animals it attacks. It can even shatter thick glass with one knockout blow.

FEMALE MAYFLY

MIGHTY SHRIMP

The mantis shrimp is fascinating for more than just its ability to knock out its lunch. Its eyes are among the most complex in the animal world. It can see ten times more colors than a human can see, and it can even see ultraviolet light. Combine its top-notch eyesight with its boxing abilities, well, now you see it—*thwack!*—now you don't.

BLACK MAMBA

4 **FASTEST MUSCLES**

Quick, flex your muscles! Too slow. The world's fastest moving muscles are found in the throats of songbirds such as the zebra finch and the European starling. To belt out some of their thrilling, trilling tunes, they must move their throat muscles a hundred times faster than the blink of a human eye.

5 **FASTEST-EATING MAMMAL**

This freaky-looking mammal has a mighty appetite! It wolfs down its food in less than a quarter of a second. That's about 227 milliseconds.

6 **FASTEST SLITHER**

This snake can slither up to 12.5 miles an hour (20 km/h), making it one of the fastest snakes in the world. And if you see one, better hope that it's slithering away from you—because its venom is deadly.

ZEBRA FINCH

STAR-NOSED MOLE

87

BUG-INSPIRED 'BOTS

PARATARSOTOMUS MACROPALPIS CAN **RUN ON CONCRETE AS HOT** AS 140 DEGREES FAHRENHEIT (60 DEGREES CELSIUS).

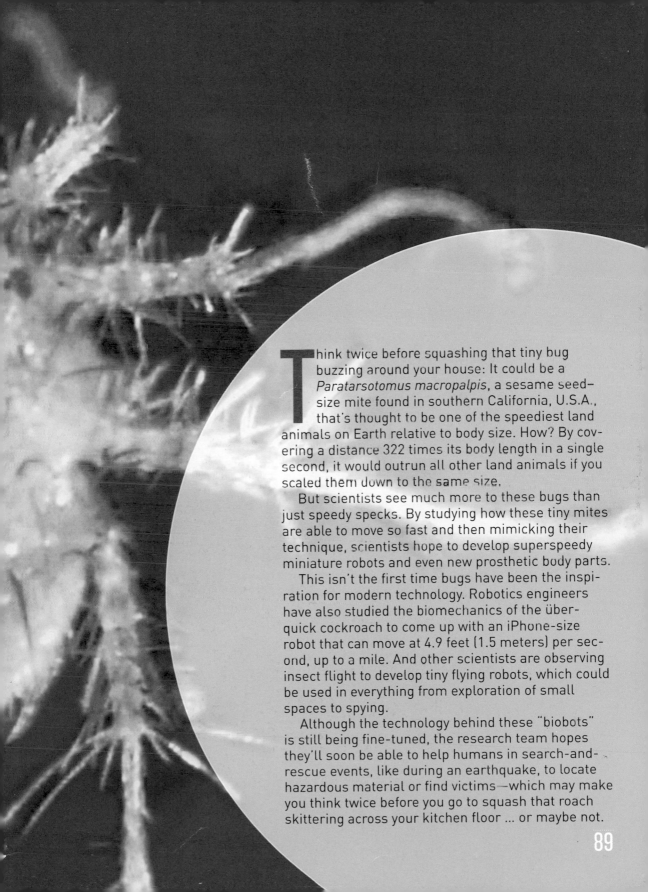

Think twice before squashing that tiny bug buzzing around your house: It could be a *Paratarsotomus macropalpis*, a sesame seed–size mite found in southern California, U.S.A., that's thought to be one of the speediest land animals on Earth relative to body size. How? By covering a distance 322 times its body length in a single second, it would outrun all other land animals if you scaled them down to the same size.

But scientists see much more to these bugs than just speedy specks. By studying how these tiny mites are able to move so fast and then mimicking their technique, scientists hope to develop superspeedy miniature robots and even new prosthetic body parts.

This isn't the first time bugs have been the inspiration for modern technology. Robotics engineers have also studied the biomechanics of the über-quick cockroach to come up with an iPhone-size robot that can move at 4.9 feet (1.5 meters) per second, up to a mile. And other scientists are observing insect flight to develop tiny flying robots, which could be used in everything from exploration of small spaces to spying.

Although the technology behind these "biobots" is still being fine-tuned, the research team hopes they'll soon be able to help humans in search-and-rescue events, like during an earthquake, to locate hazardous material or find victims—which may make you think twice before you go to squash that roach skittering across your kitchen floor ... or maybe not.

MEDAL MATCHUP

If these ten animals went paw to claw (or wing or fin) in a race, who would win?
Match the animal to its position on the podium.

3rd

9th

10th

7th

6th

PEREGRINE FALCON

SAILFISH

JACKRABBIT

GRIZZLY

90

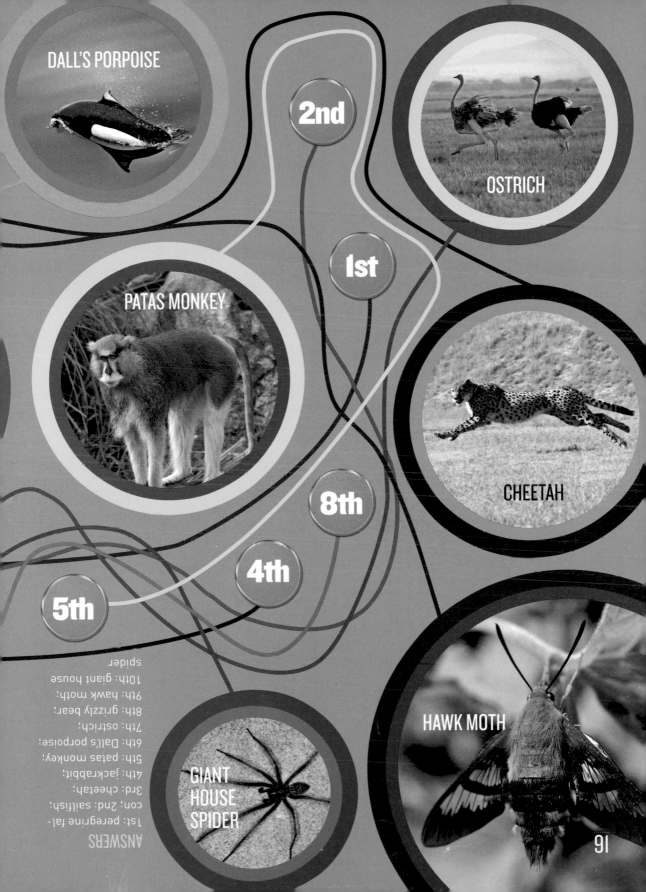

DALL'S PORPOISE

2nd

OSTRICH

1st

PATAS MONKEY

CHEETAH

8th

4th

5th

spider
10th: giant house
9th: hawk moth;
8th: grizzly bear;
7th: ostrich;
6th: Dall's porpoise;
5th: patas monkey;
4th: jackrabbit;
3rd: cheetah.
con; 2nd: sailfish;
1st: peregrine fal-
ANSWERS

GIANT
HOUSE
SPIDER

HAWK MOTH

CHAPTER 4

SLOW DOWN
AND TAKE A DEEP BREATH.
THE ANIMALS IN THIS CHAPTER
AREN'T GOING ANYWHERE.

These creatures are among the slowest species on the planet. They crawl, climb, swim, and even eat at a leisurely pace. But just because they're slow doesn't mean these animals are slacking off. They're just taking their own sweet time.

Sure, there are a lot of slow-moving animals on this planet, including snails, slugs, and sea stars that barely budge. But only one mammal is so slow that it's name actually comes from a word that also means "laziness." For that reason we crown the three-toed sloth the king of slow-mo! This hairy mammal moves at a ground speed of only about 0.1 miles an hour (0.16 km/h)—so slow that algae grows on its fur! Surprisingly, though, sloths are actually pretty good swimmers, dropping from trees into rivers and using their long arms to paddle through the water.

SCIENTIFIC NAME: **FAMILY BRADYPODIDAE**

TYPE: **MAMMAL**

LENGTH: **1.5–2 FEET (0.5–0.6 M), BODY; 2–2.4 INCHES (5–6 CM), TAIL**

THREE-TOED SLOTH

STATUS: LEAST CONCERN

LIFE SPAN: UP TO 40 YEARS IN THE WILD

HABITAT: TREETOPS IN TROPICAL FORESTS

DIET: LEAVES, BUDS, TWIGS

RANGE: SOUTH AMERICA

WEIGHT: 6.5–11 LBS (3–5 KG)

Check out these creatures that prefer life in the slow-lane.

SLOWEST
FISH

SEAHORSE

This sluggish sea creature chugs along at the slowest pace of any fish in the ocean, with some of the smaller species likely reaching up to only 0.01 miles an hour (0.016 km/h). Its awkward motion brings to mind the movement of a horse—with none of the speed.

SLOWEST
MARSUPIAL

KOALA

This tree-dwelling, herbivorous Australia native eats almost nothing but eucalyptus leaves—a high-fiber, low-protein diet that doesn't make it especially zippy! Because they are so low on energy, these super-sluggish marsupials sleep about 75 percent of the time and spend only about four minutes a day actively moving around. Now that's life in the slow lane!

SLOWEST
REPTILE

TORTOISE

Talk about a leisurely stroll! Creatures in the family Testudinidae sport large, heavy shells that make them unlikely to win any sprints. A desert tortoise, for example, can take a whole minute to walk just 10 feet (3 m)!

SLOWEST
FLAPPING INSECT

SWALLOWTAIL BUTTERFLY

Five flaps per second (300 per minute) may sound pretty fast to us, but it's actually the slowest wing beat of any insect. The pattern at the back of the butterfly's tail looks like a head, eyes, and antennae, which gives it a little extra time to escape from confused predators.

Four more slowpoke superstars
of the animal kingdom.

SLOWEST MOLLUSK

GARDEN SNAIL

What does the phrase "you're moving at a snail's pace" really mean? It means it takes you an hour at top speed to run the 50-yard (45 m) dash! Sure, that's slow, but it's not so bad for a small critter that carries its house on its back.

SLOWEST BIRD

AMERICAN WOODCOCK

Flying at 5 miles an hour (8 km/h) makes this bird a record breaker in the speed category—or rather lack thereof. The bird's lengthy bill, perfect for pulling snacks from the soil, has earned it the nickname "bog sucker."

BANANA SLUG

Did someone drop a banana on the ground? Nope, that's the banana slug, which is often yellow but can also be green, brown, or white. These slime-excreting creatures have been observed to move at a rate of up to 6.5 inches (16.5 cm) in a min-ute—now that's sluggish!

WHEEL BUG

The only insect in the United States known to sport a crest, this slow-moving assassin bug is named for the semicircular wheel-like protrusion behind its head. A beneficial garden dweller that preys on "pest" insects, the long-legged, small-headed wheel bug can pierce and immobilize prey in seconds with its toxic bite.

THE SPEED OF SIGHT

Some small animals may be speedy, but when it comes to their vision, they actually see in slow motion. Researchers have discovered that the smaller the creature, the more info it can process in a short period of time, which gives it an advantage in avoiding danger and escaping predators. Take a housefly, for example. The speed of a fly's vision is four times faster than a human's. Faster eyes lead to a slow-mo perspective, which allows the insect time to react and buzz away as a rolled up newspaper heads its way. It's no wonder you can never seem to swat those pesky bugs!

HOUSEFLY

EYE TO EYE

Faster vision means seeing the world in relative slow motion. Here's how the speed of some species' vision compares with that of humans.

HOUSEFLY: **4 TIMES FASTER**
GOLDEN-MANTLED GROUND SQUIRREL: **2 TIMES FASTER**
RHESUS MACAQUE: **1.6 TIMES FASTER**
DOG: **1.4 TIMES FASTER**
CAT: **1.1 TIMES SLOWER**
TIGER SALAMANDER: **2 TIMES SLOWER**
BLACKNOSE SHARK: **3.3 TIMES SLOWER**
LEATHERBACK TURTLE: **4 TIMES SLOWER**
EUROPEAN EEL: **4.3 TIMES SLOWER**
DEEP-SEA ISOPOD (A MARINE WOOD LOUSE):
15 TIMES SLOWER

SLOW AND STEADY
UNDER THE SEA

MANATEE

Sometimes called the "sea cow," this animal earns its nickname with its easy, steady speed. The lumbering giant usually swims about 5 miles an hour (8 km/h), which makes it one of the slowest marine mammals. But don't underestimate the manatee! If needed, it can reach up to 20 miles an hour (32 km/h) in short bursts.

SEA SPONGE

Hope this sea sponge is not in a hurry—it can move only 0.04 to 0.16 inches (1–4 mm) per day. That allows this absorbing animal plenty of time to soak in the beauty of the ocean!

SEA STAR

Sea stars can use their thousands of tiny feet to move through the ocean at more than 3 feet (1 m) per minute. If a slow getaway causes an unfriendly encounter with another animal, no problem. This crafty creature can regrow limbs—and sometimes even its entire body!

NARWHAL

This Arctic porpoise may be one of the ocean's slowest swimmers, but it shows amazing marathon-like endurance: It can take long, deep dives underwater for up to 20 minutes before surfacing for oxygen. Slow-and-steady narwhals sport a distinctive long tusk (prominent in males) up to 8.8 feet (2.7 m), earning them the nickname "unicorn of the sea."

GREENLAND SHARK

We think of sharks as swift and ready to strike at any time, but the Greenland shark swims less than 1 mile an hour (1.6 km/h). This not-so-fast fish has earned the nickname "sleeper shark" because it is so slow, it sometimes appears to be sleeping!

SEA ANEMONE

Here's a creature that usually likes to anchor itself to rocks on the ocean floor and stay put. Sometimes, however, these tentacled creatures will creep along slowly by flexing their bodies—a movement so slow it might best be captured by time-lapse photography! Sea anemones can also move by detaching themselves from the ground and inflating their bodies so they can more easily be carried by the current to a new location.

POKY PUPS

There are usually two reasons for dogs to be slow: They either have supershort legs, or they are too heavy or tiny to pick up speed. Here are some slow critters in the canine community that meet that criteria.

DACHSHUND

Hot-diggety-dog, this pup's legs are short! Although dachshunds are known to reach up to about 15 miles an hour (24 km/h) for short periods, this scrappy canine is still considered slow compared with some of its superswift hound cousins.

SKYE TERRIER

The Skye terrier's short legs keep it on the sidelines at the dog track. In fact, this rare breed gets plenty of exercise just walking around at home! These loyal pups thrive on attention and affection and can be trained for work as therapy dogs.

PEKINGESE

First brought to the West by the British in the late 19th century, this breed was a companion to nobles and members of the royal family in ancient China. At a shoulder height of *ruff*ly only 6 to 9 inches (15–23 cm), the princely puffball's short legs make it a relatively slow mover.

CLUMBER SPANIEL

Just like a little teapot, this breed of dog is short and stout. Up to 20 inches (50.8 cm) tall at the shoulder and up to 85 pounds (38.6 kg), the clumber spaniel has the ability to creep quietly and keep the barking to a minimum, which makes it a better hunting partner than jogging partner.

ENGLISH BULLDOG

Woof! Nicknamed the "sour mug," this typically sweet breed carries around its muscular 40- to 50-pound (18–23 kg) body on stocky legs in a sort of waddle. Bulldogs that overdo it with snacks may suffer from weight problems, which can contribute to their sluggish speed.

BASSET HOUND

This floppy-eared, short-limbed dog hasn't won any races lately—its legs make up less than half of its total body height and hold up to 65 pounds (29 kg) of pure pooch! Originally bred to be hunting dogs, these canines travel at a slow pace that their human companions can easily keep up with.

105

SLOW SPECIES, FAST DNA!

There's not much that's fast about the tuatara. The scaly species—a lizard-like reptile found only in New Zealand—grows slowly, moves slowly, and, well, does just about everything slowly, with one exception: Scientists say that the animals are actually evolutionary sprinters. After recovering DNA sequences from the bones of nearly 9,000-year-old tuatara fossils, scientists were able to establish the speed of DNA changes. Their discovery? The tuatara's DNA changes faster than any other animal on Earth. That was surprising news to scientists since it debunked the long-standing theory that slow-moving animals evolve slowly, too.

Scientists hope to study tuataras' DNA to discover more about evolution in humans. And because these "living fossils" can survive more than 100 years in the wild, they've got plenty of time to catch up with the critters.

TUATARAS CAN HOLD THEIR BREATH FOR UP TO AN HOUR.

TUATARAS HAVE A **THIRD EYE** ON TOP OF **THEIR HEAD.**

HOW SLOW CAN YOU GO?

Animals go head-to-head to see who's the slowest species of them all.

KOALA VS. SLOTH

WINNER

WHO SLEEPS THE MOST?

While koalas sleep approximately 18 hours a day, sloths are actually much less slothful. A recent study found that sloths in the wild sleep 9.5 hours a day, 6 hours fewer than previously thought.

GIANT TORTOISE VS. LIZARD

WHO BREATHES THE SLOWEST?

Waiting for a tortoise to exhale? Don't hold your breath! The reptiles have been observed to take just four breaths per minute, compared with lizards, whose breathing rate can be nearly ten times faster.

WINNER

WOMBAT VS. KANGAROO

WINNER

WHO DIGESTS FOOD SLOWER?

It can take up to two weeks for wombats to digest a meal, which actually comes in handy when food is scarce. Kangaroos have a much zippier digestive system, processing their chow in less than a day.

COACHWHIP VS. ROUGH-SCALED SNAKE

WHO SLITHERS SLOWER?

Not all snakes are created equal. The rough-scaled snake—a medium-size, venomous snake found in Australia—is believed to be among the slower snakes on Earth, with some estimates being as low as 1 mile an hour (1.6 km/h). It's cousin the nonvenomous coachwhip can move up to 4 miles an hour (6.4 km/h)—handy when going after prey or escaping enemies!

WINNER

3 MINUTES

SPIDER

THE RACE FOR LAST PLACE

2 MINUTES

9.58 SECONDS

EMPEROR PENGUIN

HUMAN

110

5.95 SECONDS

CHEETAH

Does slow and steady really win the race? It does if the winner is the one who is last to cross the finish line! In the battle of the slowest, here's how some species would stack up over 100 meters.

EASTERN BOX TURTLE

20 MINUTES

2 HOURS

SNAIL

WORM

1.5 HOURS

A SLOW, SLOW DINO

Scientists don't know for sure which dinosaur was the record holder in the category of slowest moving, but the *Stegosaurus* was definitely at the top of the list of poky beasts. This massive meanderer maxed out at only 3.7 miles an hour (6 km/h) for short distances—so slow that a human could have easily outrun it. The only thing a *Stegosaurus* may have done quickly is swing its spiky tail as a weapon! Why was it so slow? That question remains a mystery, but it probably had to do with its short legs and the heavy plates it carried on its back. Scientists think these mountainous plates may have been used to warn prehistoric predators to stay away or maybe to help members of the same species recognize one another.

STEGOSAURUS

LIVED DURING: **LATE JURASSIC PERIOD (150 MILLION YEARS AGO)**

LOCATION: **NORTH AMERICA**

LENGTH: **29 FEET (9 M)**

HEIGHT: **12 FEET (3.7 M)**

WEIGHT: **3.4 TONS (3 MT)**

ALBATROSS

GRAY WHALE

SLOW-AT-A-GLANCE

1

SLOWEST BIRD TO MATURE

Some birds leave the nest rather quickly, but this long-lived bird (family Diomedeidae) may take up to ten months to learn to fly—and up to ten years to become an adult! Compare that with a swallow, which begins to fly at about 20 to 25 days old, and one thing's for sure—the albatross is in no hurry to grow up!

2

SLOWEST VENOMOUS PRIMATE

The slow loris easily wins this one. That's because the nocturnal mammal that uses its wide eyes to spot prey and forage for food is also the world's only known venomous primate. When it feels threatened, the tree dweller defends itself with a megapainful bite that injects toxins into its aggressor.

3

SLOWEST WHALE

At an average speed of three to five knots, the gray whale is the slowest swimmer of all whales. It is also a master migrator, swimming in groups called "pods" more than 12,400 miles (20,000 km) each year. The whales stay close to shore and swim both night and day, taking approximately two months to make the journey.

SLOW LORIS

ELEPHANT

4 SLOWEST NEST BUILDER

Sure, most birds work hard at building their nests, but the bald eagle really takes the cake. It can spend about two weeks crafting its perfect roost! What's one reason the move-in date is so delayed? Check out chapter 1 and you'll see that this mighty bird also builds the world's biggest nest.

5 SLOWEST HEART RATE

Beating just six times per minute, the car-size heart of the blue whale is the slowest in the animal kingdom. Scientists have theorized that creatures with a slower heart rate may live longer, so maybe it's no surprise that the average life span of a blue whale is 80 to 90 years!

6 SLOWEST REACTION TIME

Not all animals can have quick reflexes and nimble movements. Because of an elephant's large size, it takes longer for it to react to stimuli. Why? Messages travel back and forth along the nervous system (from the brain throughout the body), and the longer the distance the messages have to travel, the slower an animal's reaction time. An elephant's is 100 times slower than that of a small shrew!

BALD EAGLE

BLUE WHALE

HAVE A HEADACHE?

THE GEOGRAPHIC CONE SNAIL IS THE **MOST VENOMOUS** OF THE **500 KNOWN SPECIES** OF CONE SNAIL.

TRY SOME SNAIL VENOM!

One of the world's slowest species may play a part in creating a fast-acting pain reliever. Chemists have created an experimental drug made from the venom of carnivorous cone snails, which live in the tropical waters of the Pacific and Indian Oceans. While the snails use the venom to instantly paralyze prey, scientists are hoping to put it in pill form to treat people suffering from cancer, diabetes, nerve pain, and more. The drug, which is still in development, is said to be more than 100 times stronger than some of the strongest medications available today. Now that's some powerful poison!

THERE IS NO ANTIVENOM FOR A CONE SNAIL STING.

SLOW, SLOWER, SLOWEST

Rank these animals in order of speed.

CHICKEN

SLOW ...

MOUSE

SQUIRREL

ANSWERS
Squirrel (12 miles an hour/19 km/h), chicken (9 miles an hour/14 km/h), mouse (8 miles an hour/13 km/h)

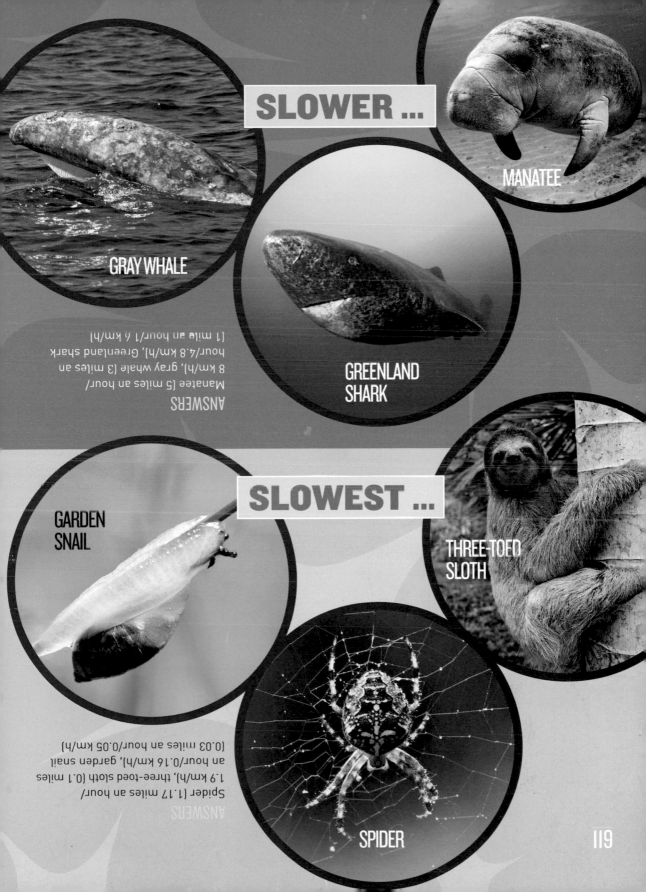

SLOWER ...

MANATEE

GRAY WHALE

GREENLAND SHARK

ANSWERS
Manatee (5 miles an hour/
8 km/h), gray whale (3 miles an
hour/4.8 km/h), Greenland shark
(1 mile an hour/1.6 km/h)

SLOWEST ...

GARDEN SNAIL

THREE-TOED SLOTH

ANSWERS
Spider (1.17 miles an hour/
1.9 km/h), three-toed sloth (0.1 miles
an hour/0.16 km/h), garden snail
(0.03 miles an hour/0.05 km/h)

SPIDER

CHAPTER 5

WHOA ... THAT SOUND WAS REALLY LOUD. WHERE—OR WHAT—DID IT COME FROM?

From the smallest insects to the biggest mammals, animals of all sizes can make noises as loud as some of the loudest sounds in the world. Whether they're attracting mates or warding off predators, these noisy creatures all have something to say.

Throughout this chapter you will see mentions of decibels (dB). These are measurements of sound. A whisper is about 30 dB; a regular conversation is about 60 dB. A sound of 120 dB (such as a siren) can cause pain, and noises of 160 dB (such as an explosive blast) can cause your eardrum to rupture—ouch!

ONLY MALE MICRONECTA SCHOLTZI MAKE THIS INTENSE SOUND.

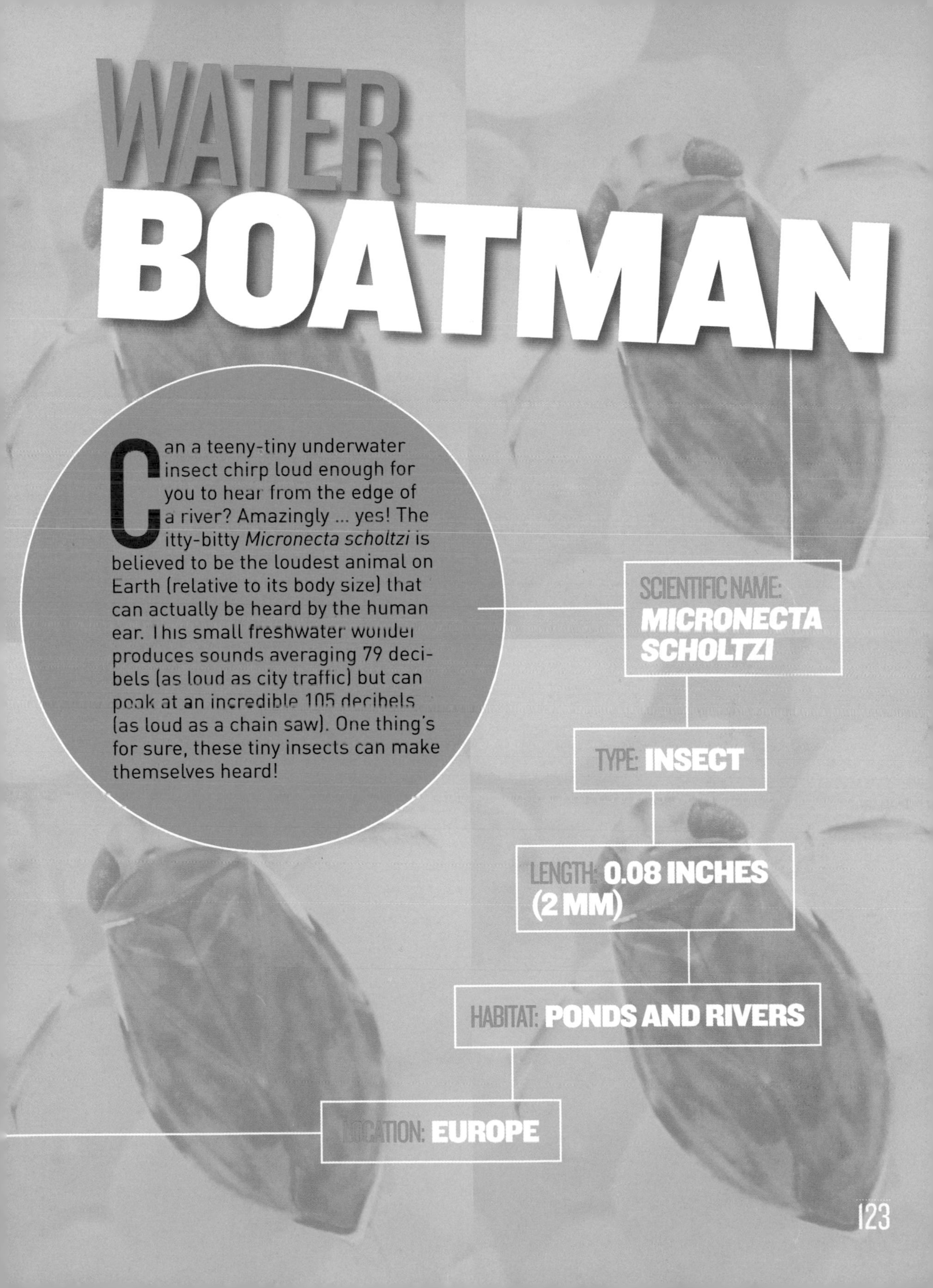

WATER BOATMAN

Can a teeny-tiny underwater insect chirp loud enough for you to hear from the edge of a river? Amazingly ... yes! The itty-bitty *Micronecta scholtzi* is believed to be the loudest animal on Earth (relative to its body size) that can actually be heard by the human ear. This small freshwater wonder produces sounds averaging 79 decibels (as loud as city traffic) but can peak at an incredible 105 decibels (as loud as a chain saw). One thing's for sure, these tiny insects can make themselves heard!

SCIENTIFIC NAME: MICRONECTA SCHOLTZI

TYPE: INSECT

LENGTH: 0.08 INCHES (2 MM)

HABITAT: PONDS AND RIVERS

LOCATION: EUROPE

THE RUNNERS-UP ...

Listen up! These record setters top the charts because of their noisy natures. See what all the clicking, chirping, howling, and bellowing is about!

LOUDEST
SUMMER VISITOR

CICADA

If you like your summers nice and quiet, this is one houseguest whose company you won't enjoy. Not only is the cicada menacing to look at, but some make a powerful clicking sound that can be heard up to a mile (1.6 km) away! When these creatures crowd in swarms of thousands, you'll be running for the earplugs, lickety-split!

LOUDEST
ULTRASONIC INSECT

BUSHCRICKET

This little creature can emit high-frequency calls of up to 110 decibels—as loud as a power saw at close range! But because much of its noise is ultrasonic (meaning it's too high-pitched to be heard by human ears), scientists use special equipment to measure the massive racket.

LOUDEST **MONKEY**

HOWLER MONKEY

Some say it howls; some say it growls. Either way, the howler monkey is the loudest land animal around! Its howls are a method of communication that humans haven't quite cracked. If you hear one of these monkey messages, don't worry: The hairy howler could still be up to 3 miles (5 km) away!

LOUDEST **MAMMAL**

BLUE WHALE

At 188 decibels, the blue whale's song is the loudest sound in the animal kingdom. This endangered creature communicates at such a low frequency, however, that it pulses, moans, and groans go largely unheard by human ears. But whales can certainly hear each other—even up to 1,000 miles (1,600 km) away.

Here are four more clamorous critters that blasted their way into the record books.

LOUDEST **BIRD**
OILBIRD

If you find yourself in a South American cave at night, bring earplugs. The clicks, shrieks, and squawks of an oilbird can reach 100 decibels at close range. Add to that a colony of thousands of oilbirds and you'll be heading for the exit in no time.

LOUDEST **BAT**
GREATER BULLDOG BAT

These mini-mammals use echolocation to track fish in rivers, ponds, and ocean surf. Emitting high-pitched (ultrasonic) sounds of up to 140 decibels, they fly close to the surface of the water and swoop down to grab the unsuspecting prey with their huge taloned feet.

LOUDEST **AMPHIBIAN**

COMMON COQUI

On a quiet and still night in Puerto Rico, listen for the male coqui. He will be the frog making sounds as loud as a hand drill all night long! This nocturnal noisemaker's distinctive calls have been recorded at 100 decibels from only a few feet (1 m) away. Just try getting some shut-eye with that racket going on!

LOUDEST **SNAP**

PISTOL SHRIMP

This sneaky shrimp wins for a supersonic *snap* that's loud enough to stun (or even kill) its prey! Its quickly closing claw shoots a jet of water at an astounding 62 miles an hour (100 km/h), forming a bubble that pops with a noise of about 200 decibels. That's louder than a rocket at blastoff!

ANIMAL
CHATTERBOXES

S cientists studying animal communication have discovered that some species' loud squawks, grunts, or chirps
may actually be a complex language
much like human speech.

After analyzing the calls of seven different
species including chickadees, finches, bats,
killer whales, and orangutans, scientists discovered that repetitions in their barks, whistles, and clicks reflect patterns similar to the
way we speak. And though these animals

aren't necessarily speaking sentences to one
another, experts believe that they likely have
a way of communicating that's purposeful
and to the point.

Some animals "talk" to each other even if
they're separated. Take lions, for example. At
dusk and dawn, they call out to fellow pride
members with bellowing roars that echo
across the plains for miles—a way for the
group to stay connected even as they split up
to hunt or to guard their territory.

RING THE ALARM

Scientists say that many kinds of animals make loud alarm calls when a predator is nearby. Here are just a few species that sound the call when faced with stranger danger.

FLORIDA SCRUB-JAY

This blue bird releases a high-pitched scream when it spots a hawk and a sharp cawing noise when it sees a cat.

PRAIRIE DOG

When a predator enters its territory, this rodent warns neighbors with a squeaky *chee chee chee* call that sounds like a dog's squeeze toy.

ELEPHANT

The supersmart pachyderm has a bunch of different warning calls, such as trumpeting and even a "bee rumble" that scientists think lets others in the herd know to buzz off when the pesky insects are nearby.

PROBOSCIS MONKEY

When a proboscis spots a predator lurking nearby, it gives others a heads up with a series of calls. The monkey's big nose helps to amplify the alarm.

And as parrots and macaws feed in the tropical treetops, they repeatedly squawk loudly to nearby birds who may be concealed in the thick leaves and flowers. Some calls are warning signals of a nearby predator, while others may just be a simple check-in with a fellow bird bud. So the next time you hear animals making a racket, you'll know that it's not just a bunch of noise!

129

THAT SOUNDED LIKE A ...

Sometimes our ears play tricks on us. These animals are known for sounding like something they're not, leaving humans scratching their heads and thinking, *Did I hear that right?*

MACHINE GUN
DAUBENTON'S BAT

The loud clicking noises of this bat are so regularly spaced that they sound like a machine gun, occurring in bursts of five to ten seconds at a time. Fortunately, this bat feeds on insects, so once you determine the source, feel free to walk fearlessly.

WOMAN SCREAMING
FOX

More than a dozen police officers in the Brisbane, Australia, suburb of Calamvale spent hours investigating a report of a woman screaming, only to discover it was actually a fox! They scoured bushlands and even used thermal imaging technology in their search for the source of the mysterious yelling.

BABY CRYING
BOBCAT

If you hear a baby crying in the woods at night, think twice before you rush to its side. That crying may be coming from a bobcat, the most abundant and widespread wild cat in the United States.

HUMAN TALKING
AFRICAN GRAY PARROT

If you're looking for a pet that will chat back when you talk to it, an African gray parrot may be a good bet. This bird mimics human voices and repeats words and phrases, often as clear as a bell, which could lead to a case of mistaken identity!

SIREN
NORTHERN MOCKINGBIRD

Songbirds like to mimic the sounds around them. But if there are no nature sounds around, what's a city bird to do? The northern mockingbird can imitate what it hears: sirens, musical instruments—even a dog barking!

HUMAN LAUGHING
HYENA

Ever found something to be so funny that you laughed like a hyena? Well, it turns out the hyena's signature sound isn't funny at all! Its eerie human-like cackle is actually a sign that the animal is frustrated—and possibly ready for a fight.

GET OUT OF MY TERRITORY

Some creatures make a racket warning intruders to stay off their turf. Check out these loud animal calls that say, "This is my stomping ground!"

RED SQUIRREL

Get too close to a red squirrel's domain, and you're likely to hear loud screeches and yips rattling through the air. These ear-piercing alarms scold the animals that come too close to the bushy-tailed rodent's stash of nuts, acorns, and other treats.

WOODPECKER

This bird's with the band! As drummer of the forest's musical ensemble, the woodpecker claims its territory by making a *tap-tap-tap* sound on trees. No trees? No problem. The woodpecker will make do with any environment it has and even drill onto other objects such as lampposts or gutters on houses.

LOON

Hoot, yodel, wail, and laugh (called a tremolo)—loons have a lot to say. When it comes to defending their territory, it's the yodel that says, "Get lost, buddy!" The hoots and wails help them locate each other, and the tremolo means they are alarmed or excited.

LLAMA

Llamas are so good at protecting their territory that they are used as guard animals on South American farms. Get too close to the llama's stomping ground and you could be met with high-pitched squeals and a forceful kick!

COYOTE

When a coyote strings together a series of blaring yips, howls, and barks, what it's really saying is the animal equivalent of "Get off my lawn!" Not only does this commotion ward off intruders, but it also lets its other coyote friends know its location.

EASTERN SCREECH-OWL

True to its name, this owl screeches to defend its nest and babies. The shrill songs make a whinnying sound that lasts up to two seconds. A trill "bounce song" called a tremolo is longer and helps family members stay in touch.

SINGING DOGS ARE EXTREMELY FLEXIBLE—THEY CAN JUMP AND CLIMB LIKE CATS!

SINGING DOGS!

These dogs sure can carry a tune! New Guinea singing dogs communicate with each other through tuneful howling. The super-rare canines—it's believed that there may be just a few left in the wild—were discovered high in the wet cloud forests of New Guinea, an island off the coast of Australia. Today, there are about 200 singing dogs living in zoos and as pets around the world.

So how does the singing dog's tune differ from a normal canine's howl? First it sounds more like a yodel, with the tones going up and down (some people say it's similar to a humpback whale's song). And when the dogs get together, they put on quite the show. If one dog starts singing, others join in, coordinating their howls and harmonizing, much like members of a pop group would. Now that's putting the wow in bowwow!

NO TWO DOGS SOUND ALIKE. EACH ONE HAS A UNIQUE VOICE.

Find out which animal has the bigger voice in the wild.

WHO'S LOUDER, ANYWAY?

ELEPHANT VS. LION

WINNER

Though a lion's roar is mighty, it can be heard from only about 5 miles (8 km) away. An elephant's foot stomping and rumbling, on the other hand, create vibrations in the ground that can travel up to 20 miles (32 km) away!

BULLFROG VS. CRICKET

WINNER

Both make plenty of noise at night, but you are more likely to pick up on the cricket's high-pitched chirps than a bullfrog's low croak. That's no small feat, considering bullfrogs are among the loudest amphibians on the planet.

CROCODILE VS. HIPPO

WINNER

Crocodiles can make some pretty mean growls when confronting a predator, but their watering-hole foes really go the distance. If they're threatened or angry, hippos release a roar that can be as thunderous as a rock band playing just 15 feet (4.6 m) away!

MAKE SOME NOISE!

Check out how these animal noises measure up to some of the loudest things in the world!

ROCK CONCERT

115 dB **=** A LION'S ROAR

= 110 dB

A JAMAICAN FRUIT-EATING BAT'S SHRIEK

CHAIN SAW

A DOG'S BARK

= 100 dB

SUBWAY TRAIN

A decibel (dB) is the unit for measuring sound. The louder the noise, the higher the decibel. For example, a crying baby is about 115 dB.

A CICADA'S CHIRP **=** **120 dB** AMBULANCE SIREN

A PIG'S SQUEAL **=** **130 dB** JACKHAMMER

A HOWLER MONKEY'S CALL **140 dB =** AIRPLANE TAKING OFF

LOUDEST DINO BLAST

Dino detectives think the fancy head crest of *Parasaurolophus* used to be quite a handy instrument! For years scientists had different ideas about its function—that it might have been a weapon, or a place to store extra air, or maybe even a snorkel. But when a scientist created a model of this dinosaur's horn, he made a cool discovery: It produced a low-pitched, deep, booming sound (like a tuba) that could have allowed adult *Parasaurolophus* to communicate over long distances. Experts even think males made different sounds than females, since males generally had longer crests. This powerful prehistoric instrument could have created (sound) waves for miles around!

PARASAUROLOPHUS

LIVED DURING: LATE CRETACEOUS PERIOD (75 MILLION YEARS AGO)

LOCATION: NORTH AMERICA

WEIGHT: 4 TONS (3.6 MT)

LENGTH: 33 FEET (10 M)

HEIGHT: 16 FEET (5 M)

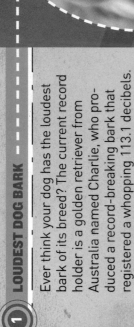

GOLDEN RETRIEVER

AFRICAN ELEPHANT

LOUD-AT-A-GLANCE

1 LOUDEST DOG BARK

Ever think your dog has the loudest bark of its breed? The current record holder is a golden retriever from Australia named Charlie, who pro- duced a record-breaking bark that registered a whopping 113.1 decibels. It blew away the previous record set by a German shepherd in London, whose bark registered a measly 108 decibels.

2 LOUDEST KITTY CAT

If there's an angry African lion around, you're likely to know about it. Lions communicate with a variety of noises, including thunderous 110-decibel roars they use to show ownership and defend territory. Nice kitty!

3 LOUDEST STOMP

The stomp of an elephant's foot com- bined with its vocal rumblings can create ground vibrations that can travel 20 miles (32 km). That's one way to get your point across! Elephants actually have a variety of calls they use to communicate and express themselves. A growl might mean "Hi, there!" and a bellow might mean "Ouch!" or "I'm scared." Screaming means "Help!" and, along with their famous trumpeting, "Back off!"

AFRICAN LION

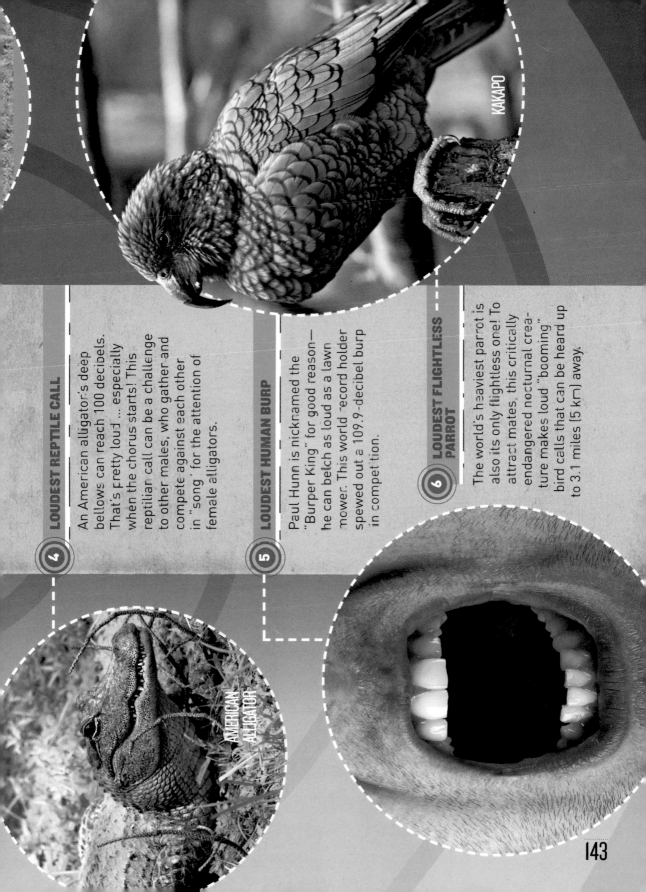

KAKAPO

4 LOUDEST REPTILE CALL

An American alligator's deep bellows can reach 100 decibels. That's pretty loud ... especially when the chorus starts! This reptilian call can be a challenge to other males, who gather and compete against each other in "song" for the attention of female alligators.

5 LOUDEST HUMAN BURP

Paul Hunn is nicknamed the "Burper King" for good reason—he can belch as loud as a lawn mower. This world-record holder spewed out a 109.9-decibel burp in competition.

6 LOUDEST FLIGHTLESS PARROT

The world's heaviest parrot is also its only flightless one! To attract mates, this critically endangered nocturnal creature makes loud "booming" bird calls that can be heard up to 3.1 miles (5 km) away.

AMERICAN ALLIGATOR

WHISTLING A NEW TUNE!

Among all of the animals in the sea, dolphins are certainly the chattiest: They constantly communicate with each other using whistles and clicks (also known as echolocation) that can be very loud. And now, scientists are close to discovering just what all of that noisy chitchat is about.

Working with a pod of wild dolphins in the Caribbean, experts taught them certain whistles associated with words for food and toys. Then, using special software on an underwater computer that matches dolphin-speak with English, they set out to translate those whistles—which can be up to ten times higher than the highest pitch a human can make out—into words. One day, while observing the pod, one of the dolphins whistled, and the software registered "sargassum," a type of seaweed. It was a match—and the first real-time translation of a dolphin whistle.

Although the software is still a prototype, scientists are closer to understanding dolphin's natural language—and possibly one day even communicating with them in the wild.

BOTTLENOSE DOLPHINS CAN MAKE UP TO 1,000 CLICKING NOISES PER SECOND.

DOLPHINS HAVE A SIGNATURE WHISTLE THEY USE TO IDENTIFY THEMSELVES — KIND OF LIKE A NAME!

FUN AND GAMES

SAY WHAT?

Who made that noise? Match the sound to the species!

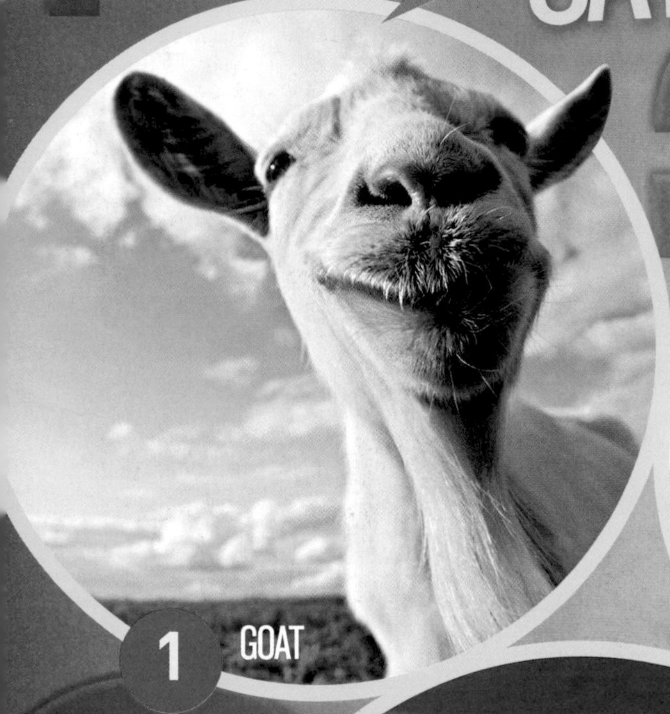

1
GOAT

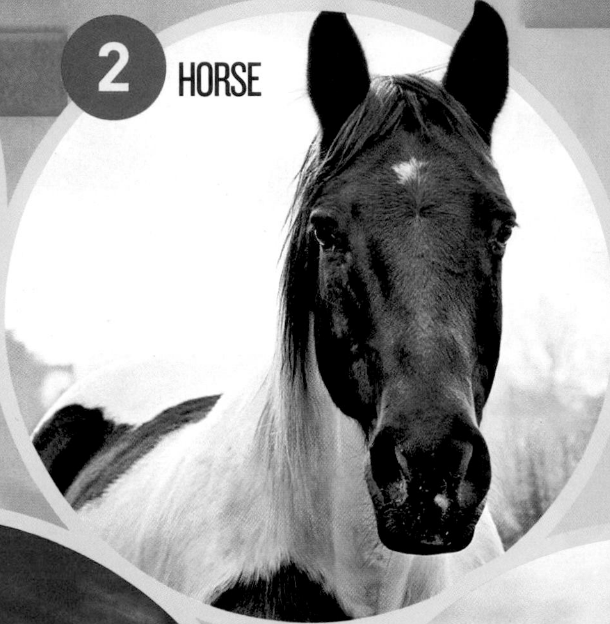

2
HORSE

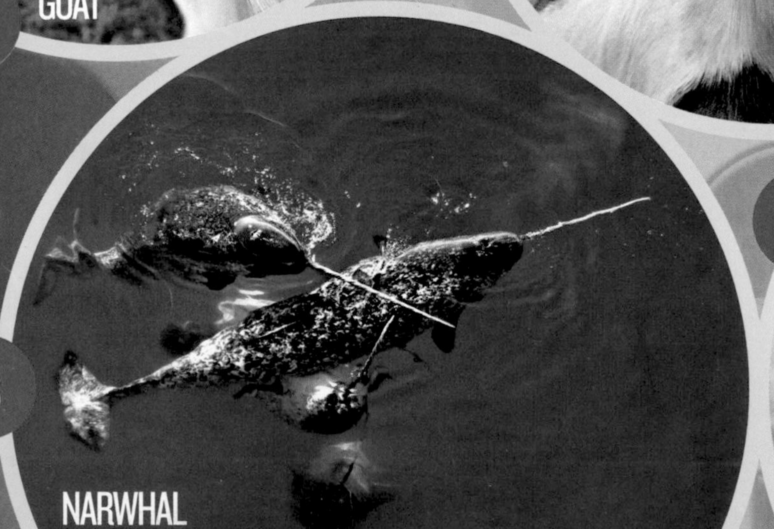

3
NARWHAL

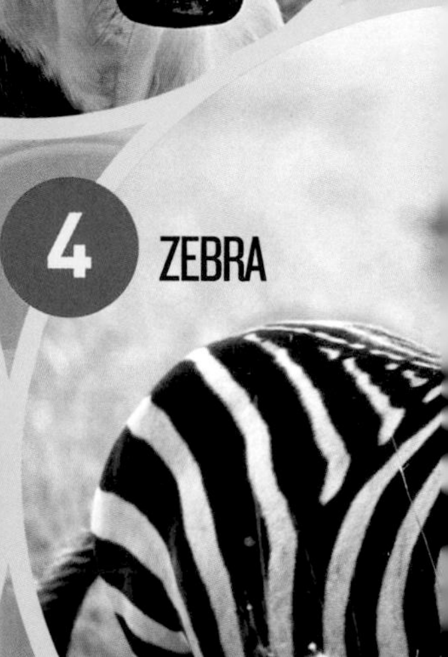

4
ZEBRA

A GROAN

B WHINNY

C SCREAM

D BLEAT

ANSWERS: 1: D; 2: B; 3: H; 4: G; 5: E; 6: F; 7: A; 8: C; 9: I

5 PIGEON

DONKEY **6** **7** WALRUS

8 **9** KANGAROO

KOALA

E **COO** F **BRAY** G **WHOOP** H **SQUEAL** I **GRUNT**

CHAPTER 6

EACH AND EVERY ANIMAL IS WEIRD IN ITS OWN SPECIAL WAY.

The animals in this chapter have been crowned king because they look so zany, or act strangely, or boast bizarre features. What will be your favorite oddball animal? Flip the page to explore the wild world of weird.

BLOBFISH

SCIENTIFIC NAME: **PSYCHROLUTES MARCIDUS**

TYPE: **FISH**

LENGTH: **12 INCHES (30.5 CM)**

DIET: **CRUSTACEANS**

HABITAT: **DEEP SEA WATERS**

RANGE: **SOUTH PACIFIC**

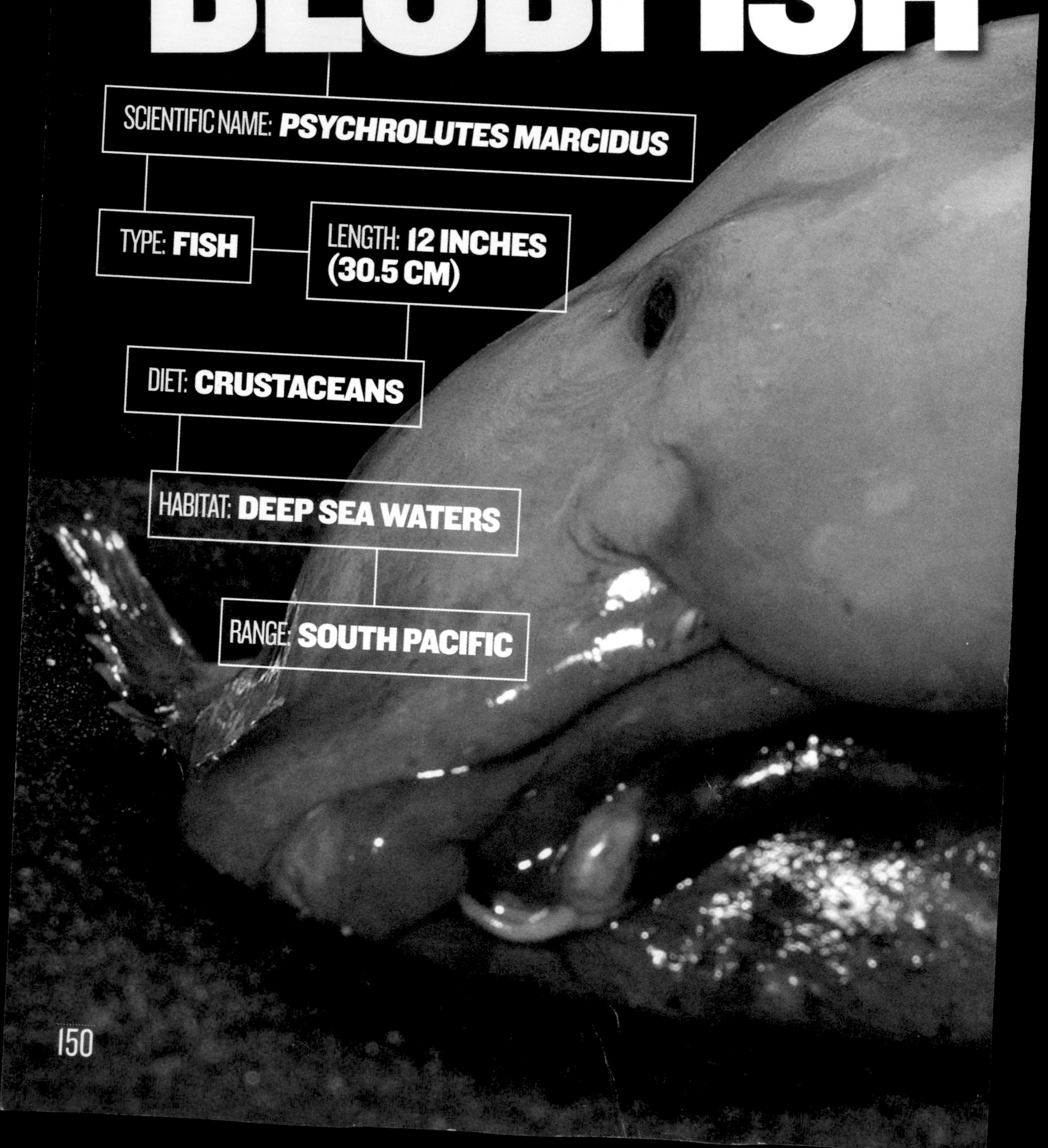

Looking like a cartoon character that's part grumpy face, part gelatin mold, the blobfish is the official mascot of the Ugly Animal Preservation Society. Some call it hideous, others marvel at its unique features, and a few even think it's downright adorable. These blobs can mostly be found in deep waters off the coast of Australia, bobbing around at ocean depths of about 2,000 to 4,000 feet (610–1,220 m) and chowing down on lobsters and crabs.

BLOBFISH HAVE REALLY SOFT BONES. THIS HELPS KEEP THEM FROM CRACKING UNDER THE EXTREME PRESSURE OF OCEAN DEPTHS.

THE RUNNERS-UP ...

When rounding up the weirdest of the weird, don't forget to corral these creatures into the mix. Their wacky looks and unusual behavior have earned them a spot in the "strangest sea life" category!

LEAFY AND WEEDY SEA DRAGONS

Keep an eye out for the seaweed off the southern coast of Australia. You just might be looking at a fish! Closely related to seahorses, sea dragons sport a weedy exterior that makes them true masters of camouflage. Even weirder, it's the male sea dragons that carry the eggs before hatching, not the females.

DUMBO OCTOPUS

The dumbo octopus may be an awkward-looking animal, but it uses a graceful dance to get from place to place. The big-finned cephalopod gets its name from Dumbo, Disney's big-eared, flying elephant character. Unfortunately this octopus is a rare site—it has been known to live as far as 13,000 feet (3,962 m) below the ocean's surface, making it the deepest living octopus in the world.

ANGLERFISH

It you're diving in the deep sea and think you see a firefly, don't be fooled. It could be a female anglerfish trying to lure its prey. This fiendish fish boasts a blue-green light that dangles in front of its face and lights up through a chemical process called biolumines-cence. The glowing light is the perfect lure for curious prey and makes the rest of the fish's body—including its large mouth and sharp teeth—almost disappear in the dark ocean.

HAGFISH

How did the hagfish get the nickname "snot eel"? By gagging its predators with slime! While a predator thinks it's biting down on a surefire supper, the hagfish spews out slime from tiny pores all over its body. The stunned attacker almost always releases and moves on—a trick that has kept the hagfish thriving for 300 million years!

MORE RUNNERS-UP ...

Look to the land to find these outrageous oddballs. Their unconventional mugs just might knock you off your feet!

NAKED MOLE RAT

Colonies of big-toothed, blind mole rats live 6 feet (1.8 m) underground in a cooperative social structure that's more like groups of insects than rodents. Dozens and dozens of these homely, hairless male creatures dig burrows, gather food, or tend to one dominant female: their queen.

SUN BEAR

This bear loves honey so much it has a superlong tongue perfect for slurping the sweet snack. So why is it called the "sun bear" and not the "honey bear"? Legend has it that the bib-shaped marking on its chest was thought to look like the rising sun. Funny name for a nocturnal animal!

SPINY ORB WEAVER

This freaky, spiky spider likes to hang out in shrubs and at the edges of forests. The strange spines on its back come in red, orange, and yellow varieties; some orb weavers even have colored legs. The last thing the mama spider does is lay up to 260 eggs—but then she dies before meeting her oddball brood.

SUPERB BIRD OF PARADISE

Talk about a bunch of show-offs! Male superb birds of paradise perform a wacky dance around female birds to display their perky plumage. To go with their elaborate feathery display (called a breast shield), the males let out a series of loud shrieks—just to make sure they're noticed!

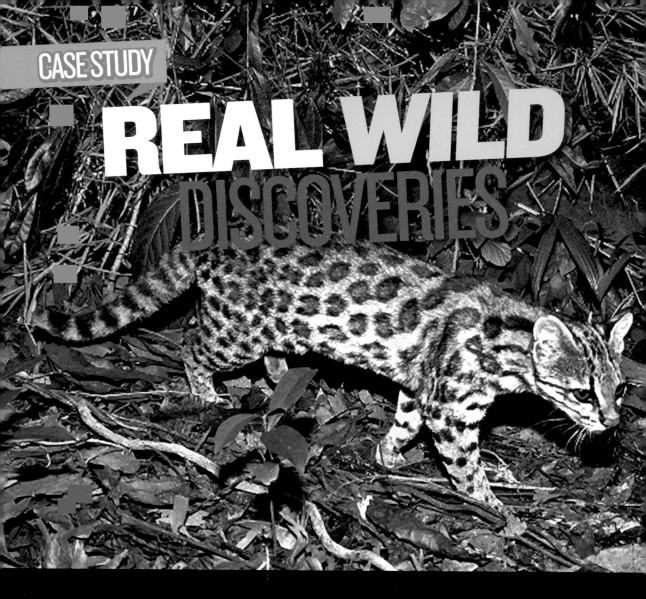

REAL WILD
DISCOVERIES

In the wild, you never know what you're going to find! Take these researchers, for example, who were studying the evolution of wild cats in the Amazon when they identified a brand-new species of kitty. The southern tigrina—about the size of a house cat—looks a lot like a mini-leopard and lives exclusively in the forests of southern Brazil. After analyzing DNA samples of similar-looking cats, the researchers determined that this elusive animal is its own species, not part of another cat family as originally thought.

The tigrina isn't the only out-there species found accidentally. Scientists in Antarctica unexpectedly found strange sea anemones in the ice shelf. Believed to be the only sea anemones to live in ice, they spend their entire life hanging upside down! The researchers were actually testing their underwater equipment when they spotted thousands of these invertebrates burrowed upside down in the ice. How's that for a turn of events?!

OTHER ODD FINDS!

Check out the weirdest new species in town!

What:
Vampire frog

Where:
Thailand

Date of Discovery: 2008

Why It's Weird:
With fangs and an appetite for birds, this blood-sucker is one fearsome frog!

What:
Illacme plenipes millipede

Where:
California, U.S.A.

Date of Discovery:
Rediscovered in 2005

Why It's Weird:
This millipede has 750 legs and is believed to be the leggiest creature on Earth.

What:
Olinguito

Where:
Colombia and Ecuador

Date of Discovery: 2013

Why It's Weird:
This nocturnal mammal with a teddy bear face is the first new species of carnivore discovered in the Western Hemisphere in more than three decades.

RARE ANIMAL ODDITIES

Some of Earth's quirkiest creatures may be in danger of disappearing forever. Take a look at some of nature's dwindling populations and find out which have been deemed vulnerable, threatened, or endangered by scientists.

DUGONG
STATUS: VULNERABLE

Also called the "sea cow," the dugong lives in the warm coastal waters of the Red Sea and the Indian and Pacific Oceans and faces threats from human activity. Thought to be an inspiration for sailors' tales of mermaids, this relative of the elephant perches its tail underwater to keep its head above the surface.

NORTH ISLAND BROWN KIWI
STATUS: ENDANGERED

The wings of this flightless puffball are hidden under its spiky feathers. Found only in New Zealand, the country's national bird can outrun a human, even though it's only about the size of a chicken! The funky creature is endangered due to habitat loss and the introduction of predators into its habitat.

PURPLE FROG
STATUS: ENDANGERED

First discovered in 2003, this freaky frog spends most of its time 12 feet (3.7 m) underground in burrows, emerging for only a few weeks a year to mate. The puffed-up visitor uses its touch-sensitive nose to find termites and then sucks them up with its tongue. A major threat to this species is loss of its forest habitat to crop cultivation.

AYE-AYE
STATUS: ENDANGERED

At first scientists thought this oddball animal was a rascally rodent, but today they know it's actually a peculiar primate—the largest nocturnal primate on Earth. The aye-aye's long fingers (especially its even longer middle digit) help it pick its favorite meal, insect larvae, out of tree cavities. Its population is on the decline, however, because habitat destruction means fewer and fewer trees for the animal to dig into.

HOODED SEAL
STATUS: VULNERABLE

Whether its trying to impress a mate or show potential foes who's boss, the male hooded seal can inflate its nasal cavity, or "hood," until it looks ready to burst. These seals live in Arctic and North Atlantic waters, with moms giving birth to their pups on ice floes. Those shrinking habitats are making the hooded seal population shrink, too.

AXOLOTL
STATUS: CRITICALLY ENDANGERED

About the size of a teacup, an axolotl sports feathery gills and a cartoon-like face that makes it a delightfully odd sight. This salamander lives in the lakes near Mexico City, Mexico, which are being threatened by pollution and drainage. It's a rare treat to come across this happy-looking water lover.

ANIMAL MASH-UPS

These animal mash-ups are mesmerizing mammals that are either the result of animal parents from different species, or they just look like they are! See if you can tell the difference!

SAIGA

Looking like a sheep-antelope hybrid, the droopy-nosed saiga are actually all antelope. Saiga may travel up to 72 miles (116 km) a day during migration season to get from their summer grasslands to their winter desert homes.

ZONKEY

When two animals in the horse family are mixed, there are many possible combinations. A zonkey, also known as a zeedonk, is a mixed-up-looking half zebra, half donkey. In fact, any equine (such as a horse or donkey) mixed with a zebra is called a zebroid.

SAVANNAH CAT

This odd-looking cat is half domestic Siamese cat and half serval, a wild animal native to African grasslands. The loyal and affectionate kitty likes to play fetch and is a faithful follower to its owner.

CHEVROTAIN

Also known as the mouse deer, this world's smallest hoofed animal is aptly nicknamed for its deer-like features. It's 4.4-pound (2 kg), 1.6-foot (50 cm) body has a tiny version of the stomach feature that a deer has, allowing it to regurgitate its partially digested food.

WHOLPHIN

What do you get when you cross a female bottlenose dolphin and a male false killer whale? A wholphin, of course. This hybrid animal is so rare that the only known wholphin that exists right now in captivity lives at a sea park in Hawaii.

CAMA

Scientists were hoping to create an animal with the strength, patience, and endurance of a camel and the highly desirable wool of a llama. They were successful in creating the first ever live hybrid between New World camelids (the llama) and Old World camelids (the camel) in 1998 with the birth of "Rama the cama." Several more have been bred since.

FREAKY FEATURES!

These animals may look odd, but some of their unique adaptations and peculiar parts actually help them survive in the wild.

Found In:
Central and South America

Freaky Features:
Translucent wings

How They Help: See-through wings make this insect appear like a flying work of art. But they're not there just to look pretty: The wings make it hard for predatory birds to track the butterfly in flight.

GLASSWINGED BUTTERFLY

BACTRIAN CAMELS CAN CHUG 30 GALLONS (114 L) OF WATER IN JUST 13 MINUTES.

BACTRIAN CAMEL

Found In:
Central and East Asia

Freaky Features:
Large, squishy foot pads

How They Help: Described as "bags filled with slime," this two-humped camel's foot pads help it stay upright in an extreme terrain. The pads act like snow-shoes, keeping the camel from sinking into the sandy desert.

LONG-BEAKED ECHIDNA

Found In:
New Guinea

Freaky Feature:
Long, narrow snout

How It Helps: This spike-covered critter's beak and long sticky tongue help it slurp up hard-to-reach food such as worms and ants, and special cells in its bill are sensitive to the electric fields surrounding all living things. Scientists think that the echidna is the only land mammal to have the ability to search for food this way.

BABY ECHIDNAS ARE CALLED **PUGGLES.**

Both are oddball organisms, but which is wackier?

WHO'S WEIRDER?

ZOMBIE WORM VS. TENTACLED SNAKE

WINNER

TENTACLED SNAKE

Why it's weird: The only snake species sporting twin "tentacles" on the front of its head, it's thought to be able to detect prey and lure fish with the odd attachments.

ZOMBIE WORM

Why it's weirder: Producing an acid that dissolves bones, it resides in decomposing fish and whale skeletons on the ocean floor.

LESSER SHORT-TAILED BAT VS. "YODA BAT"

"YODA BAT"

Why it's weird: This tube-nosed fruit bat bears an uncanny resemblance to the big-eared Jedi Master from the Star Wars movies.

LESSER SHORT-TAILED BAT

Why it's weirder: Using its rolled-under wings as forelegs, it's one of only two species of bat that walks on the ground.

WINNER

SATANIC LEAF-TAILED GECKO vs. LEGLESS LIZARD

LEGLESS LIZARD

Why it's weird:
Spending most of its time underground, it may live its entire life within an area no bigger than your dining room table!

SATANIC LEAF-TAILED GECKO

Why it's weirder: This lizard lives to blend in, sporting a speckled brown body and a tail resembling a rotting leaf that it can suddenly shed to fool a predator.

WINNER

HERO SHREW vs. SOLENODON

HERO SHREW

Why it's weird:
A sturdy spine gives this mini-mammal amazing strength: It is reportedly able to withstand the weight of a full-grown man on its back.

SOLENODON

Why it's weirder: This rare, rabbit-size, uncommonly venomous mammal injects its prey with toxins through its teeth.

WINNER

THE WEIRD **WILD**

0.6
inches
(16 mm)

Size, in diameter, of a Philippine tarsier's eyeball, about the same as a marble— and bigger than its brain.

5
feet
(1.5 m)

Approximate maximum length of the rare markhor goat's giant corkscrew-looking horns.

4,265

feet
(1,300 m)

Depth at which you may find the ghoulish goblin shark swimming in the ocean.

5

Number of main arms of a basket star, which branch off into a multitude of twisty tendrils that ensnare food such as plankton.

2

Number of heads on a tortoise found in South Africa, likely the result of a rare genetic mutation.

REAL-LIFE BIG

Does the creature known as Bigfoot actually exist? Once upon a time, it may have! Scientists think the *Gigantopithecus* may have been the closest real-life equivalent to that mythical beast. Fossils of the polar bear–size ape have been found in Asia (including India, China, and Vietnam) and show that it is related to the modern orangutan. Studies of the beast's pitted, cavity-riddled teeth reveal that it had a hankering for bamboo. It must have taken a huge amount of bamboo to satisfy a beast that weighed as much as three gorillas!

NAME: GIGANTOPITHECUS

LIVED: FROM 1 MILLION TO 300,000 YEARS AGO

LOCATION: ASIA

WEIGHT: 1,200 POUNDS (544 KG)

HEIGHT: 10 FEET (3 M)

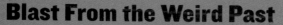

Blast From the Weird Past

Chalicotherium ▲
Looking like a cross between an ape and a donkey trying to stand upright, the knuckle-walking wonder called *Chalicotherium* could have reached high into trees and swiped at leaves and branches. Although its head was horselike, it had claws on its feet instead of hooves.

Arthropleura ▲
This nearly 10-foot-long (3 m) centipede-like creature roamed North America about 300 million years ago with few or no predators to keep its population at bay. Scientists have still not found the mouth fossil of this alarming arthropod, so no one knows if it had terrifying teeth.

FOOT

Gastornis ▶
This odd beast had tiny, useless wings and a giant beak that it used to crack open seeds and fruits. The fossils of the menacing 6.5-foot-tall (2 m) bird had scientists originally thinking that it was a dangerous predator. But they recently found out that the gentle giant probably preferred hunting for plant life.

BIRD-DROPPING SPIDER

MOTH

ODD-AT-A-GLANCE

1 WEIRDEST CAMOUFLAGE

If you were a spider, how would you get other animals to leave you alone? Disguise yourself as bird poop! That's exactly what the bird-dropping spider does. While the spider is very good at keeping predators away, it's also a skilled hunter. It hangs from leaves or twigs and releases an odor that attracts its favorite meal: moths.

2 WEIRDEST ADAPTATION

Wouldn't it be cool if your body could produce its own sunscreen? If you were a hippo, it could. The only catch? That sunscreen looks like blood! The hippo's body actually makes ooze that shields it from the sun's ultraviolet rays and even gives protection from some bacteria that can cause diseases. Luckily for hippos, the sweat fades to brown when exposed to air.

3 WEIRDEST DIET

The *Hemiceratoides hieroglyphica* moth of Madagascar has one weird diet. It likes to drink the tears of sleeping birds on the island. The act may look a bit creepy, but the birds don't seem to be in pain or even wake up when the moth takes its sneaky sips.

HIPPO'S "BLOOD SWEAT"

KOALA

4 WEIRDEST HIBERNATOR

Many frogs dig deep into the soil to hibernate for the winter, but the spring peeper isn't such a great digger. Instead, it finds a nice crack in a log or burrows into leaf litter. While its surroundings may freeze, the frog's body makes its own antifreeze to keep it protected. The frog's heart might stop, making it appear dead, but come spring—it springs back to life!

5 WEIRDEST BABY

Barely 0.018 ounces (0.5 g) when it is born, the koala lives inside its mother's pouch and chows on milk and "pap," a liquefied form of its mother's poop! This soupy substance contains microorganisms the koala will need to be able to eat eucalyp-tus leaves when it gets older.

6 WEIRDEST SEA MONSTER

If you ran into a monkfish in the ocean, its huge head and wide mouth might seem the stuff of scary monster legends. But some people actually choose to run into it—on a restaurant menu! It's a delicacy that some people pay top dollar to eat.

SPRING PEEPER

MONKFISH

171

THE SECRET OF THE MOLE

NAKED MOLE RATS ARE NOT MOLES AND THEY'RE NOT RATS. **THEY'RE MORE CLOSELY RELATED TO CHINCHILLAS, GUINEA PIGS, AND PORCUPINES.**

RAT!

NAKED MOLE RATS CAN LIVE UP TO 30 YEARS, MAKING THEM THE LONGEST LIVED OF THE RODENTS.

The über-creepy naked mole rat may look like it's on its last leg, but this creature is quite healthy. How so? Scientists think it's immune to cancer, has superstrong bones, and stays mentally sharp throughout its entire life—rarities in the animal kingdom.

In fact, it's this rodent's unique ability to stave off cancer that researchers hope can help us learn more about fighting the disease in the human population—and living longer lives. Labs around the world are studying the blind, hairless animal, which can live up to 30 years (about ten times longer than the life span of its relatives mice and rats), to uncover just what it is that makes this creature so darn durable.

One possibility is a protein found in mole rat tissues that prevents cells from multiplying and forming tumors. By investigating this protein and how it functions in the rat's body, scientists hope to find new ways of preventing cancer in humans, too.

WEIRD BUT TRUE ANIMAL IQ!

TRUE OR FALSE

I. Scientists are working on **making fabric** out of **hagfish slime.**

2. Jumping spiders have **two eyes** and **poor vision.**

3. There's an **odd new underwater species** that look like **mushroom-shaped jellyfish.**

4. The shoebill, **a large bird** resembling a stork, is named for its **shoe-like feet.**

5. Chinchillas take **long baths** in rivers to clean their thick fur.

HAGFISH

CHINCHILLA

JUMPING SPIDER

SHOEBILL

ANSWERS 1. TRUE. A team of researchers is hoping to create an eco-friendly material out of the hagfish's defensive slime. **2. FALSE.** Jumping spiders actually have eight eyes and are skilled visual predators. **3. TRUE.** Discovered off the coast of Australia, this species looks like mushrooms but feels like Jell-O. **4. FALSE.** It's named for its large shoe-shaped beak. **5. FALSE.** Chinchillas keep their coats clean and shiny by rolling around in dust and dirt.

CHAPTER 7

WARNING: THE ANIMALS IN THIS CHAPTER ARE THE DEADLIEST ON EARTH.

What does "deadliest" really mean? In the animal world, it can mean being the craftiest or most venomous predator. Or it can mean being a champ at defending your territory at all costs. No matter the method, one thing's for sure—you'll want to stay far away from these lethal creatures.

MOSQUITO

SCIENTIFIC NAME: **ANOPHELES**

TYPE: **INSECT**

LENGTH: **UP TO 0.6 INCHES (16 MM)**

WEIGHT: **UP TO 0.000088 OZ (2.5 MG)**

HABITAT: **WIDE VARIETY; MOST SPECIES PREFER WET AREAS**

RANGE: **WORLDWIDE, EXCEPT ANTARCTICA**

LIFE SPAN: **UP TO TWO WEEKS IN NATURE**

When it comes to the world's deadliest creature, surely a meaty, big-toothed, fierce-looking beast takes the trophy, right? Wrong. The truth is that the animal that causes hundreds of thousands of human deaths every year is smaller than a paper clip and—with no heft or huge claws—can land on your arm without you even noticing. How is that possible? Often inconspicuous mosquitoes can carry deadly diseases such as malaria, which are transmittable to humans through the insects' tiny bites. When malaria invades the body, it induces high fever, chills, and other flu-like symptoms in an infected person and can be fatal if left untreated. Out of the more than 3,000 species of mosquitoes, only the females of the *Anopheles* genus can transmit human malaria; in 2012, there were more than 200 million cases of malaria, with 90 percent of malaria deaths occurring in Africa. Different mosquito species also carry diseases that could be fatal without proper medical care, such as encephalitis, yellow fever, and West Nile virus.

THE RUNNERS-UP ...

Here are more lethal creatures vying for the position of top predator. Check out their killer instincts.

BOX JELLYFISH

This super-deadly jellyfish is so venomous that its smallest victims are instantly stunned or killed. The stings attack the heart and nervous system, and human survivors have reported permanent scarring and intense pain for weeks after an attack. That's mighty powerful for a creature that reaches only up to 4.4 pounds (2 kg).

ASSASSIN BUG

Acanthaspis petax injects its prey with a venom that paralyzes it in a matter of seconds. It then dissolves and softens the prey's guts and sucks them out until only an empty shell remains. The assassin bug even wears the dead bodies of its ant conquests on its own back to confuse predators.

STONEFISH

The stonefish is aptly named for its ability to camouflage itself to look like stone. Combine that with the fact that it's also the world's most venomous known fish, and you've got yourself one scary sea creature. Just one sting can be fatal to humans, who have been known to accidentally step on the frightening fish when out for a leisurely swim.

HIPPOPOTAMUS

These vegetarians are not interested in an animal meal, but when these 7,000-pound (3,175 kg) beasts charge at another animal, the hippo enters the ranks of the deadliest animals on Earth. Hippos fiercely defend their territory and are reportedly responsible for more human deaths than any other large animal in Africa.

MORE RUNNERS-UP ...

Here are more of the deadliest hunters, biters, and stingers on Earth. Find out how they go in for the kill.

FISH EAGLE

This bird doesn't have X-ray vision, but it has the next best thing. It can perch in high trees and see down through water with great clarity—and that makes no fish close to the surface safe from its high speed, feet-first dive into the water to grab its prey. The bird is such a good hunter it needs to spend only about ten minutes per day actively looking for food. Now that's an animal that eats from the "fast food" menu!

POISON DART FROG

Don't say the frog didn't warn you! This amphibian is one of many animals that sports warning colors: brightly colored bodies that are a signal to other animals to stay away. Why? This tiny terror secretes enough toxin from its skin to kill ten humans.

GREAT WHITE SHARK

The great white shark leaves little left of its dinner. When this 10-foot-long (3 m) fish bites down on its prey, it pushes 4 tons (3.6 mt) of pressure through every square inch of its teeth. While the great white packs a deadly bite, the number of people killed by the animal remains low, with far more shark deaths per year caused by humans than human deaths caused by sharks.

GEOGRAPHIC CONE SNAIL

Being stung by this sea dweller almost always means certain death. Just one drop of its highly toxic venom will paralyze the victim immediately and kill it within minutes—including humans. But the Indo-Pacific reef inhabitant is not all bad; its venom is being researched as a massively potent painkiller.

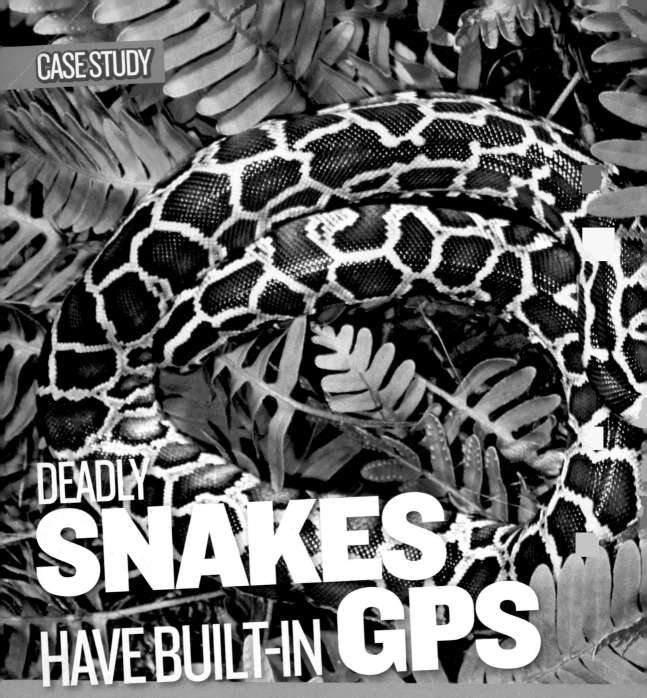

DEADLY SNAKES HAVE BUILT-IN GPS

There's no place like home—especially if you're a Burmese python. The deadly snake, which can suffocate and swallow deer and alligators whole, is said to be able to find its way back to a familiar environment, even after being moved miles away.

To test the snakes' sense of direction, scientists captured and fitted 12 of them with tracking devices. They then released half the pythons where they had been captured and the other half in locations more than 20 miles (32 km) away. They observed and recorded that the snakes released at a distance made their way back toward where they had been captured! The pythons

184

SUPER SENSES!

Here's how other predators use senses to track their prey:

Smell: Sharks rely on their keen sense of smell to sniff out their next victims. They can locate their prey from hundreds of feet away.

Taste: Monitor lizards flick their forked tongues in and out to "taste" the air and to capture scent particles that send a message to their brain telling them if prey is nearby.

Touch: Star-nosed moles have noses that feature 22 tentacles (each with about 25,000 touch receptors) that can touch as many as 12 objects per second—allowing them to quickly identify and eat worms, insects, and small fish.

Hearing: A fox has such sensitive ears that it can hear the underground noises of small mammals. When it has located its prey, the fox digs it up.

Vision: Birds of prey have extraordinary eyesight. A red-tailed hawk can spot a mouse from 100 feet (30.5 m) above.

demonstrated a homing instinct—a sort of internal map and compass—that had not before been documented in a snake species.

These resolute reptiles aren't just returning to their homes because they like the accommodations: Scientists believe they might be returning to the spot where they think hunting is best. Now those are some smart snakes!

Members of the animal kingdom have some mighty gruesome methods for catching their prey or warding off threats.

KILLER INSTINCTS

DEATH BY DROWNING

After lying in wait like a statue for as long as it takes, the crocodile quickly lunges at birds and small mammals. It pulls its surprised prey into the water to drown and dismember it. Crocodiles also hunt larger mammals and are thought to cause an estimated 1,000 human deaths each year.

DEATH BY STOMPING

Even an herbivore needs some deadly defenses up its sleeve. For the elephant, it's stomping. Elephants kill an estimated 500 people a year worldwide. And if a 14,000-pound (6,350 kg) beast on top of you is not enough of a crushing blow, the elephant's sharp tusks can be deadly tools in their own right.

DEATH BY SWIPING

Warning: Stay away from an angry polar bear. Even when it is not looking for its favorite meal of seal meat, a polar bear can rip an animal in two with just one swipe of its mighty paw. One reason for attack? To protect its cubs.

DEATH BY CHOMPING

The piranha has interlocking teeth as sharp as razors. That's bad news for unsuspecting fish or any animal on the menu of these aggressive omnivorous packs. Don't worry, though. Attacks on humans are rare for these South American river dwellers.

DEATH BY CONFUSION

Black eagles can confuse and disorient their prey in all kinds of ways. They will sometimes cleverly keep their prey from seeing them by flying directly into the sun and then swooping in on the unsuspecting meal. They like to feast on small mammals and the eggs and young of other birds. From this animal, expect the unexpected.

DEATH BY ELECTROCUTION

Talk about a shocker! The electric eel can deliver up to 600 volts of electricity to its fish and amphibian prey. That's five times as strong as a standard U.S. wall socket! Though human deaths from these animals are rare, their shocks can cause heart failure and drowning.

SERIOUSLY SNEAKY SNAKES

Not all snakes are deadly, but these sure are. Read on to discover how these slithering snakes sneak up on their unsuspecting victims.

BLACK MAMBA

With a head the shape of a coffin, this snake practically screams "deadly"! Its potent venom is so fast acting that unsuspecting prey often don't know what hit them. The snake gets its name from its black mouth, even though its body is gray.

KING COBRA

The king cobra is the longest of all venomous snakes and can grow up to 18 feet (5.5 m) long. Its venom packs a powerful punch that can kill an animal as large as an elephant. That's a tall order, even for a snake that can "stand up" to the height of a full-grown man!

OLIVE-BROWN SEA SNAKE

This underwater (but also air-breathing) snake preys on fish eggs, fish, crustaceans, and mollusks. Its venom breaks down the nerves and muscles of its victims, making digestion a snap.

SIDEWINDER

The sidewinder is literally up to its eyeballs in camouflage! It spends most of its time lying in sand with only its head peeking out to watch for unsuspecting prey.

ANACONDA

It's not all death-by-venom in the snake world. The anaconda grips its prey with an ever tightening squeeze, suffocating its victim and swallowing it whole. Weighing about 550 pounds (250 kg), the green anaconda is pound-for-pound the world's largest snake, which means there's a whole lot of reptile behind that powerful grip.

INDIAN COBRA

The Indian cobra prefers to prey on lizards, frogs, and rodents, but it won't hesitate to bite a person encountered in its search for food. Along with several other varieties of poisonous snake in Asia, the Indian cobra is responsible for tens of thousands of human deaths each year.

SPIDER

SMALL

CRICKET

BUT
DEADLY

Some of the smallest—and most lethal—predators on the planet can fit right in the palm of your hand (not that you'd want them to)!

TERMITES

Predator: Velvet worm
Prey: Crickets, spiders, and termites
Size: Up to 8 inches (20.3 cm)
Deadly Details: This critter immobilizes its prey with a gooey substance that it squirts out from glands on its head. Using its jaws to puncture its victim, the predator then injects it with digestive saliva and sucks out its liquefied insides.

CRAB

Predator: Blue-ringed octopus
Prey: Crabs and mollusks
Size: 5 to 7.8 inches (12.7–19.8 cm)
Deadly Details: The blue-ringed octopus injects a highly toxic venom into the water or directly into its prey. The venom of this cephalopod quickly causes paralysis and can lead to death if the toxin affects the respiratory system or heart. An accidental bite could be fatal to a human in minutes!

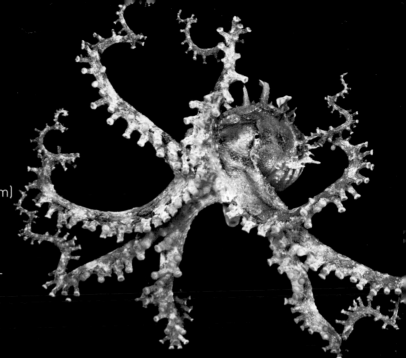

Predator: Jewel wasp
Prey: Cockroaches
Size: Up to 0.9 inches (2.3 cm)
Deadly Details: This insect uses senses in its stinger to inject venom directly into its victim's brain. The poison paralyzes the cockroach, allowing the wasp to lay an egg on its abdomen. When the egg hatches, the larva eats its way into the belly of the bug and feeds off its internal organs.

COCKROACH

Predator: *Malo kingi* (common kingslayer)
Prey: Small fish
Size: Bell up to 1.2 inches (3 cm)
Deadly Details: This tiny jellyfish is armed with a massive amount of poison: Its slings are said to be powerful enough to kill a human, making it one of the most venomous creatures in the world. The species is named after Robert King, a tourist who was killed by the deadly jelly while swimming in Australia.

FISH

If these animals met in the wild, who would wind up the winner?

ULTIMATE ANIMAL MATCHUPS!

STOAT VS. RABBIT

WINNER

A 10-inch-long (25.4 cm) stoat can kill a rabbit ten times its size. After identifying its prey, the stoat performs a kind of distracting dance for the rabbit—hopping and thrashing and rolling about. Moving ever closer to its captive audience, it eventually ambushes its target, chasing down the rabbit and delivering a fatal bite to the back of its neck.

CAPE BUFFALO VS. LION

The lion may be the most ferocious animal on the savannah, but if caught off guard, the big cat might just be bested by the giant buffalo. When one Cape buffalo saw another facing certain doom, it charged head-on into the attacking big cat and used its two sharp horns to flip it more than 16 feet (5 m) into the air!

WINNER

ANACONDA VS. JAGUAR

Jaguars may be strong and stealthy with some of the sharpest claws on the planet, but the powerful anaconda—which can grow as long as a limousine—can clobber the big cat hunting for fish in the water. With one quick chomp on the jaguar's neck, the anaconda can wrap its body around the big cat, squeezing it until it suffocates ... and becomes dinner.

WINNER

GREAT WHITE SHARK VS. ORCA

They're not called killer whales for nothing: The superstrong orcas—which are actually part of the dolphin family—stun the sharks by ramming them with their big bodies at full speed, or they bring the full force of their tails down on them. In both cases the whale reportedly flips and holds the shark upside down, rendering it helpless until it suffocates.

WINNER

PREDATOR
PROGRESS REPORT

How often do these lethal beasts vanquish their prey?
Check out their "kill rates" to find out. See which
predators made it to the top of the class
in our just-for-fun grading scale.

A

Predator: Dragonfly
Prey: Flies and
other tiny insects
Kill Rate: 95%

B

Predator: African
wild dog
Prey: Gazelles,
warthogs, small
mammals, and birds
Kill Rate: 80%

C-
Predator: Great white shark
Prey: Seals, sea lions, dolphins, rays, and fish
Kill Rate: 50%

D
Predator: African lion
Prey: Wildebeests, impalas, zebras, giraffes, buffalo, and wild hogs
Kill Rate: 25%

D
Predator: Golden eagle
Prey: Rabbits, medium-size rodents, other birds, and reptiles
Kill Rate: 20%

B-
Predator: Red fox
Prey: Squirrels, rabbits, and mice
Kill Rate: 70%

D
Predator: Wolf
Prey: Elk, deer, caribou, and moose
Kill Rate: 25%

THE DEADLIEST DINO

TYRANNOSAURUS REX

Possibly the most menacing beast of the prehistoric age, the *T. rex* had a bite that was about three times as powerful as a lion's. And it's no wonder, with 60 sharp teeth, each up to 8 inches (20 cm) long. How do scientists know *T. rex* was such a killer? The proof is in the petrified poop. Fossilized dung of the prehistoric beast contains remains of its unfortunate victims, showing that it could crunch through the bones of some big beasts.

LIVED DURING: LATE CRETACEOUS PERIOD, 65 MILLION YEARS AGO

LOCATION: NORTH AMERICA

WEIGHT: 16,000 POUNDS (7,257 KG)

SIZE: 40 FEET (12 M) LONG, 20 FEET (6 M) TALL

Deadly Honorable Mentions

T. rex earned its deadly badge of honor, but these prehistoric beasts were also something to fear.

Kronosaurus is named after the myth of the Greek god Kronos, who devoured his children. This aquatic savage of the early Cretaceous period had strong jaws and teeth that could crush and shatter shells in one swift crunch.

The **Utahraptor** used its colossal claws to carry out its attacks. Fancy kicking and clawing moves were possible because of the *Utahraptor*'s long tail, which allowed it to balance like an acrobat.

KRONOSAURUS

UTAHRAPTOR

DEADLY-AT-A-GLANCE

LYNX

TARSIER

1 DEADLIEST UNDERDOG

This stealthy cat may be small and solitary, but neither size nor nature keeps it from making a big kill. The tiny 3-foot-long (0.9 m) kitty can take down prey as large as a deer.

2 MOST PAINFUL STING

Meet the world's largest wasp, which stings and paralyzes huge tarantula spiders so it can lay eggs on them. Humans have reported that this wasp has one of the most painful stings of any insect in the world.

3 CUTEST KILLER

The better to see you with! Sporting the biggest eyes relative to body weight of any mammal, this nocturnal primate uses them to find and focus on its insect prey. Once the meal is in its reach, the forest-dwelling tarsier pounces, capturing its meal with both hands. Yikes!

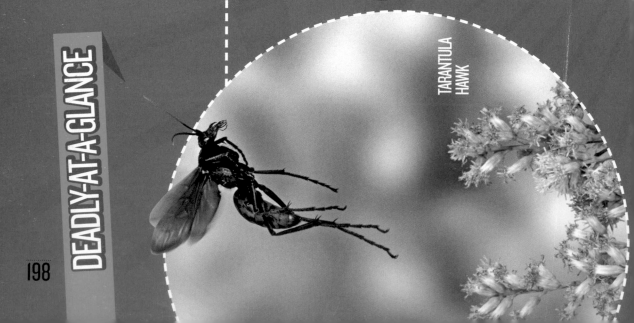

TARANTULA HAWK

SOUTHERN CASSOWARY

4 BIGGEST APPETITE

Predatory carnivores that consume up to 50 pounds (27.2 kg) of meat in one sitting, lions eat large animals including antelope, wildebeest, and zebra. The females of the pride do most of the hunting in small teams (though the males eat first!), generally heading out at night to stealthily stalk and attack their prey.

5 DEADLIEST SCORPION

As one of the world's deadliest scorpions, it may also win a prize for best restraint. Despite it's massive power, it stings only as a last resort and prefers to eat small insects.

6 DEADLIEST KICK

Although the cassowary boasts razor-sharp claws and one of the strongest kicks in the animal kingdom, it is mostly a peaceful animal. Just don't move in on the territory of this 130-pound (59 kg), 5.5-foot (1.7m) rain forest bird or you might get a kick you won't soon forget!

LION

INDIAN RED SCORPION

MANGROVE
SNAKE

MORE THAN
100,000
ANIMALS
PRODUCE **VENOM.**

THE VALUE OF VENOM!

SCORPION

BEE

Venom may be nature's most efficient killer, but scientists are discovering that it may actually bring a big boost to our health. Researchers are taking toxins from poisonous animals and studying them in the hope of healing people with diseases such as cancer and multiple sclerosis.

Medicine derived from venom has already been developed to treat diabetes and heart disease. And now, lab results show that proteins found in **bee, snake, and scorpion venom** slow growth of cancer cells or even destroy them. Using a synthetic medication

similar to venom, researchers have been able to slow the growth of cancer cells in a lab and hope that it might bring a cure for the deadly disease one day.

And cancer's not the only thing toxins treat. Other studies suggest that a substance in black widow spider venom could help fight Alzheimer's disease, while a tarantula's toxin may improve muscle activity among those with muscular dystrophy. Some people may soon feel relief from chronic pain with the help of a scorpion's sting—meaning the very stuff that could kill you may also save your life.

DEADLY
DEFENSES

Match the animal to its defense mechanism.

B OPOSSUM

1. SPEWING STINKY VOMIT

3. SHOOTING BLOOD FROM ITS EYE

5. INJECTING VENOM FROM ITS TEETH

2. PLAYING DEAD

4. SLIMING ITS ENEMIES

6. SPRAYING BOILING FLUID FROM ITS REAR

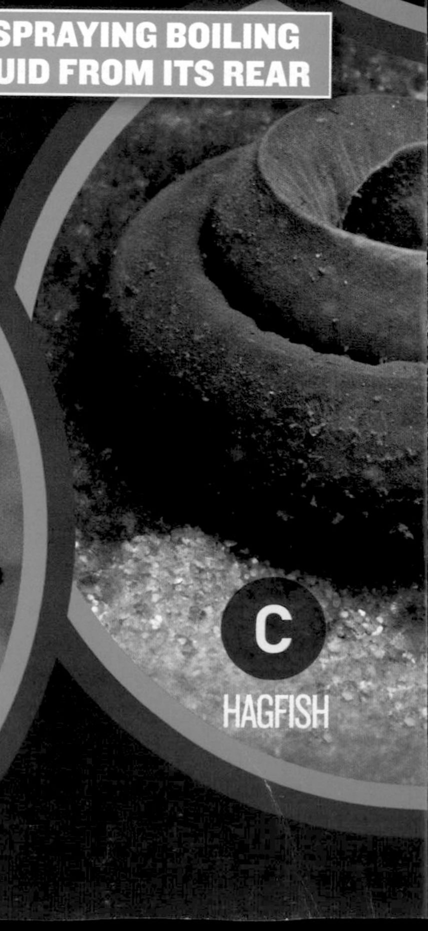

A TEXAS HORNED LIZARD

C HAGFISH

D
GILA MONSTER

E BOMBARDIER BEETLE

F VULTURE

ANSWERS
1:F, 2:B, 3:A,
4:C, 5:D, 6:E

INDEX

Boldface indicates illustrations.

ILLUSTRATION CREDITS

DRMS: DRMS; GI: Getty Images; MP: Minden Pictures; NGC: NGC; SS: Shutterstock

Front cover: (CTR), ZSSD/MP; (UPRT), © dieKleinert/Alamy; (LOLE), Hidekazu Kubo/MP; (LORT), Johan Swanepoel/SS **Spine:** ZSSD/MP **Back Cover:** (UPRT), Shevs/SS; (CTR LE), © WaterFrame/Alamy; (LOLE), © Photowitch/DRMS

Front matter: 1 (CTR), © Silksatsunrise/DRMS; 2 (CTR), © Stefan Pircher/DRMS; 4 (LE1), © Isselee/DRMS; 4 (LE2), Jan Martin Will/SS; 4 (LE3), © Woraphon Banchobdi/DRMS; 4 (LE4), © Svetlana Foote/Alamy; 4 (LE5), suebg1 photography/GI; 4 (LE6), © Sekarb/DRMS; 4 (LE7), paulrommer/SS; 5 (RT1), © roblan/DRMS; 5 (RT2), © Glenn Nagel/DRMS; 5 (RT3), © Isselee/DRMS; 5 (RT4), DnDavis/SS; 5 (RT5), © Leerobin/DRMS; 7 (CTR) 86 © Photoshot Holdings Ltd / Alamy **Chapter 1:** 8 (CTR), © Elena Elisseeva/DRMS; 10 (CTR), © Science Photo Library/Alamy; 12 (CTR), © Robert Hardholt/DRMS; 13 (UPLE), © Pete Oxford/Nature Picture Library; 13 (CTR RT), Ministry of Fisheries via GI; 13 (LOLE), © Zhitao Li/DRMS; 14 (CTR), © Photoshot Holdings Ltd/Alamy; 14 (LOLE), ©Roberto Rinaldi/Nature Picture Library; 15 (CTR RT), © Mark Moffett/MP; 15 (LOLE), © Rod Williams/Nature Picture Library; 16 (CTR), © iStock/cezars; 17 (UP), Mauricio Handler/NGC; 17 (CTR), AP Photo/Mark Bussey; 17 (LO), NOAA; 18 (UP), © Adam Gryko/DRMS; 18 (UPRT), © Scratchart/DRMS; 18 (BCKD), xpixel/SS; 18 (LOLE), © Mitsuaki Iwago/MP; 19 (UPRT), © Chmelars/DRMS; 19 (UPLE), © Dr. pramod Bansode/DRMS; 19 (CTR RT), © Salazkin Vladimir/DRMS; 19 (LOLE), © Jean-edouard Rozey/DRMS; 20 (UPLE), © Paul Banton/DRMS; 20 (CTR), © Edwin Giesbers/Nature Picture Library; 20 (LOLE), © Doug Perrine/Nature Picture Library; 21 (UPLE), AP Photo/Tsunemi Kubodera of the National Science Museum of Japan, HO; 21 (CTR RT), Kenneth Lilly/GI; 21 (LO), © Ernie Janes/Nature Picture Library; 22 (CTR), © Ryu Uchiyama/Nature Production/MP; 23 (CTR), © Yukihiro Fukuda/Nature Picture Library; 24 (UPLE), © Valeria Head/DRMS; 24 (UPRT), © Vladimir Melnik/DRMS; 24 (LOLE), © Johannes Gerhardus Swanepoe/DRMS; 24 (LORT), © Life on white/Alamy; 25 (UPLE), © Suhentu/DRMS; 25 (UPRT), © Eugene Bochkarev/DRMS; 25 (CTR LE), © Isselee/DRMS; 25 (CTR RT), © Andy Rouse/Nature Picture Library; 25 (LOLE), © Bill O'neill/DRMS; 25 (LORT), © Katrina Brown/DRMS; 26-27 (CTR), © David B. Fleetham/Seapics.com; 26 (UP), © Jaysi/DRMS; 26 (CTR LE), © Neil Wigmore/DRMS; 26 (LO), © Kalin Nedkov/DRMS; 27 (UP), © Andreanita/DRMS; 27 (UP CTR RT), © Tom Stack/Alamy; 27 (CTR RT), © Andy Rouse/Nature Picture Library; 27 (LO CTR RT), © Svetlana Foote/Alamy; 27 (LORT), © Jolka100/DRMS; 29 (CTR), Franco Tempesta; 30 (UPLE), © Orionmystery/DRMS; 30 (UPRT), © Mikelane45/DRMS; 30 (LOLE), © Markus Varesvuo/Nature Picture Library; 30 (LORT), © Bert Folsom/Alamy; 31 (UP), © Don Mammoser/Alamy; 31 (LOLE), © Friedrich von Horsten/Alamy; 31 (LOCTR), © David Tipling/Nature Picture Library; 31 (LORT), © Nick Upton/Nature Picture Library; 32 (CTR), © WaterFrame/Alamy; 34 (UPLE), © Bryan and Cherry Alexander/Nature Picture Library; 34 (CTR RT), © Joe Blossom/Alamy; 34 (LOLE), © Ingo Arndt/Nature Picture Library; 34 (LO CTR), © Bruno D'Amicis/Nature Picture Library; 35 (UPLE), © Ingo Arndt/Nature Picture Library; 35 (UPRT), © Bruno D'Amicis/Nature Picture Library; 35 (CTR LE), © Yvette Cardozo/Alamy; 35 (CTR RT), © Yvette Cardozo/Alamy; 35 (LOLE), © Joe Blossom/Alamy; 35 (LORT), © Bryan and Cherry Alexander/Nature Picture Library **Chapter 2:** 36 (CTR), Fred Kraus; 38 (CTR), Science PR/GI; 40 (CTR), © Kevin Elsby/Alamy; 41 (UP), Fred Kraus; 41 (CTR LE), WENN/Newscom; 41 (CTR RT), Brian Keller; 41 (LO), ©

Tim Graham/Alamy; 42 (CTR), Hal Beral/Visuals Unlimited Inc; 42 (LE), EPA/Darrin Vanselow/Newscom; 43 (LO), National News/
Zuma Press/MCT/Newscom; 43 (RT), Merlin D Tuttle/GI; 44 (CTR), © Richard Austin/REX USA; 45 (UP), Howie Williams; 45 (CTR),
Jennifer Plombon; 45 (LO), © WENN/Newscom; 46–47 (BCKD), Roland Birke/GI; 46 (LOLE), Steve Gschmeissner/SPL/Getty
Image; 46 (UPRT), Visuals Unlimited, Inc./Robert Pickett/GI; 47 (UPRT), Ed Reschke/GI; 47 (CTR), Roland Birke/GI; 47 (LORT),
Laguna Design/GI; 48 (CTR), © Maudem/DRMS; 48 (CTR LE), © Wafuefotodesign/DRMS; 48 (LORT), © Pablo Hidalgo/DRMS; 49
(UPLE), © Goncaloferreira/DRMS; 49 (UPRT), © David Hosking/Alamy; 49 (LORT), © Nyker1/DRMS; 50 (CTR), RB McCormack/
Australian Aquatic Biological/www.aabio.com.au; 52 (UPLE), Scott Camazine/GI; 52 (UPRT), © Melinda Fawver/DRMS; 52 (LOLE),
© blickwinkel/Alamy; 52 (LORT), © doc-stock/Alamy; 53 (UPLE), © Marvin Dembinsky Photo Associates/Alamy; 53 (UPRT), ©
Arco Images GmbH/Alamy; 53 (CTR LE), Michael DeYoung/Design Pics/GI; 53 (CTR RT), Anna Yu/GI; 53 (LOLE), © Papilio/Alamy;
53 (LORT), © Rob Walls/Alamy; 54 (UPLE), © Martin Valigursky/DRMS; 54 (UPRT), © Peter Spirer/DRMS; 54 (CTR LE), © Steven
J. Kazlowski/Alamy; 54 (CTR RT), © Jose Barcelo/DRMS; 54 (LOLE), © Jan Pokorn/DRMS; 54 (LORT), © Winzworks/DRMS; 54
(CTR), OTHK/GI; 55 (UPLE), © Gert Hochmuth/DRMS; 55 (UPRT), © ARCO/Nature Picture Library; 55 (UP CTR LE), © Johnfoto/
DRMS; 55 (UP CTR RT), © Alex Mustard/Nature Picture Library; 55 (LO CTR LE), © Steven Crabbé/DRMS; 55 (LO CTR RT), ©Tom
Brakefield/Exactostock-1491/SuperStock; 55 (LO), Stargazer/SS; 57 (CTR), Franco Tempesta; 58 (UPLE), John T. Fowler; 58
(UPRT), © Lucila De Avila Castilho; 58 (LO), © Tom Vezo/Nature Picture Library; 59 (UP), © Johannes Gerhardus Swanepoe; 59 (LOLE), © Pete Oxford/MP; 59 (LORT),
Nina E Fatouros PhD; 60 (CTR), © Gustavo Andrade/DRMS; 61 (CTR RT), Dr. Alper Bozkurt; 62 (UPLE), Tim Fitzharris/MP; 62 (UPRT), Bates Littlehales/NGC; 62 (LOLE),
Joel Sartore/NG Creative; 62 (LORT), Erlend Haarberg/Nature Picture Library; 63 (UPLE), Tim Laman/NGC; 63 (UPRT), © Tim Laman/Nature Picture Library; 63 (CTR LE),
Mitsuhiko Imamori/MP; 63 (LOLE), George Grall/NGC; 63 (LORT), Michael & Patricia Fogden/MP **Chapter 3:** 64 (CTR), © Zuzana Randlova/DRMS; 66 (CTR), © Arco
Images GmbH/Alamy; 68 (CTR), ZSSD/MP; 69 (UP), © Ole Jorgen Liodden/Nature Picture Library; 69 (CTR), © John Saunders/DRMS; 69 (LO), © Mark MacEwen/Nature
Picture Library; 70 (CTR), © Slew11/DRMS; 70 (LO), © Ron Niebrugge/Alamy; 71 (LE), © Chris & Monique Fallows/Nature Picture Library; 71 (RT), © Whitcomberd/
DRMS; 72 (CTR), Chris Johns/NGC; 73 (UP), © Miroslav Hlavko/DRMS; 73 (LO), © Sekarb/DRMS; 74–75 (BCKD), Inaki Relanzon/Nature Picture Library; 74 (CTR), © David
J. Green - animals/Alamy; 74 (UPLE), © Philip Dalton/Nature Picture Library; 74 (CTR RT), © Avico Ltd/Alamy; 74 (LO), © roblan/DRMS; 75 (UP), © Mrfiza/DRMS; 75
(CTR), Nature's Images/GI; 76 (CTR), © Melvinlee/DRMS; 76 (UPRT), © john t. fowler/Alamy; 76 (CTR LE), © Premaphotos/Alamy; 76 (LORT), © Georgette Douwma/
Nature Picture Library; 77 (CTR LE), © Stephen Frink Collection/Alamy; 77 (LORT), © Sue Daly/Nature Picture Library; 78 (CTR), © Konrad Wothe/Nature Picture Library;
80 (UPLE), J & C Sohns/GI; 80 (UPRT), EPA/Erik S. Lesser/Newscom; 80 (LOLE), © Mircea Costina/DRMS; 80 (LORT), © Teekaygee/DRMS; 81 (UPLE), © Chris Turner/
DRMS; 81 (UPRT), paulrommer/SS; 81 (CTR LE), © Matauw/DRMS; 81 (CTR RT), © AfriPics.com/Alamy; 81 (LOLE), © Elena Titarenco/DRMS; 81 (LORT), © Hanne & Jens
Eriksen/Nature Picture Library; 82 (UPLE), © Dave Bredeson/DRMS; 82 (UPRT), suebg1 photography/GI; 82 (CTR), © Suzi Eszterhas/MP; 82 (LOLE), © Grafvision/DRMS;
82 (LORT), © Woraphon Banchobdi/DRMS; 83 (UPLE), © Krystian Maj/ZUMA Press/Newscom; 83 (UP CTR), © Glenn Nagel/DRMS; 83 (CTR LE), © Ferrero-Labat/
Auscape/MP; 83 (CTR RT), © Isselee/DRMS; 83 (LO), © Isselee/DRMS; 85 (CTR), Franco Tempesta; 86 (UPLE), © Vibe Images/Alamy; 86 (UPRT), © Photoshot Holdings
Ltd/Alamy; 86 (LO), © imageBROKER/Alamy; 87 (UPRT), suebg1 photography/GI; 87 (LOLE), © Ashley Whitworth/DRMS; 87 (LORT), Visuals Unlimited, Inc./Ken Catania/
GI; 88 (CTR), Jonathan Wright and Grace Wu; 90 (UPLE), © Steven Oehlenschlager/DRMS; 90 (UPRT), © Chris & Monique Fallows/Nature Picture Library; 90 (LOLE), ©
Volodymyr Byrdyak/DRMS; 90 (LORT), © Linda Bair/DRMS; 91 (UPLE), © Todd Pusser/Nature Picture Library; 91 (UPRT), © Janina Kubik/DRMS; 91 (CTR LE), ©
Photoquest/DRMS; 91 (CTR RT), © Bob Suir/DRMS; 91 (LOLE), © blickwinkel/Alamy; 91 (LORT), © Jackeroo/DRMS **Chapter 4:** 92 (CTR), © Jaroslav Moravcik/DRMS; 94
(CTR), © Staffan Widstrand/Nature Picture Library; 96 (CTR), © Subsurface/DRMS; 97 (UP), © Andras Deak/DRMS; 97 (CTR), © RGB Ventures/SuperStock/Alamy; 97
(LO), © Crispi/DRMS; 98 (UP), © Sergio Hayashi/DRMS; 98 (LO), Visuals Unlimited, Inc./Steve Maslowski; 99 (UP), LehaKoK/SS; 99 (CTR), © John Cancalosi/Alamy; 100
(CTR), © Vinesh Kumar/DRMS; 101 (UPLE), © Aliaksandr Mazurkevich/DRMS; 101 (CTR LE), © Tom Wang/DRMS; 101 (LOLE), © Doug Perrine/Nature Picture Library;
101 (LORT), © Michael Patrick O'Neill/Alamy; 102 (UP), © Naluphoto/DRMS; 102 (CTR), © Anthony Land/DRMS; 102 (LO), © Vilainecrevette/DRMS; 103 (UP), Paul
Nicklen/NGC; 103 (CTR), © Nature Picture Library/Alamy; 103 (LO), © Andy Nowack/DRMS; 104–105 (CTR), © Ksenia Raykova/DRMS; 104 (UPRT), © Waldemar
Dabrowski/DRMS; 104 (CTR LE), © Idamini/Alamy; 104 (LORT), © Roughcollie/DRMS; 105 (UPLE), © Tkatsai/DRMS; 105 (CTR RT), © blickwinkel/Alamy; 106 (CTR), ©
Mark Carwardine/Nature Picture Library; 108 (UPLE), © Andras Deak/DRMS; 108 (UPRT), Cuson/SS; 108 (LOLE), © Marek Jelinek/DRMS; 108 (LORT), © Colin Moore/
DRMS; 109 (UPLE), Susan Flashman/SS; 109 (UPRT), © Kjuuurs/DRMS; 109 (LOLE), © Barbara Magnuson/Larry Kimball; 109 (LORT), © Robert Valentic/Nature Picture
Library; 110–111 (CTR), © Bob Suir/DRMS; 110 (UPLE), jps/SS; 110 (LOLE), Jan Martin Will/SS; 110 (LORT), © Evgenyatamanenko/DRMS; 111 (UPLE), Jiri Hera/SS; 111
(UPRT), DnDavis/SS; 111 (LO), Melinda Fawver/SS; 113 (CTR), Franco Tempesta; 114 (UPLE), © Pete Oxford/Nature Picture Library; 114 (UPRT), © Mark Carwardine/
Nature Picture Library; 114 (LO), © Ian Butler/Alamy; 115 (UP), john michael evan potter/SS; 115 (LOLE), Richard Lowthian/SS; 115 (LORT), © Patricio Robles Gil/Sierra
Madra/MP; 116 (CTR), Dave Wrobel/GI; 118 (UPLE), © Elena Elisseeva/DRMS; 118 (UPRT), © Lukas Blazek/DRMS; 118 (LO), © Taophoto/DRMS; 119 (UPLE), © Sue
Flood/Nature Picture Library; 119 (UPRT), © Greg Amptman/DRMS; 119 (UP CTR), © Nature Picture Library/Alamy; 119 (LOLE), © Bruce Macqueen/DRMS; 119 (LO
CTR), © Mircea Costina/DRMS; 119 (LORT), © Vilainecrevette/DRMS **Chapter 5:** 120 (CTR), Anton_Ivanov/SS; 122 (CTR), CB2/ZOB/WENN.com/Newscom; 124 (CTR), ©
Steve Byland/DRMS; 125 (UP), © Skynetphoto/DRMS; 125 (CTR), EBFoto/SS; 125 (LO), Larry Foster/NGC; 126 (UPRT), © Tui De Roy/Nature Picture Library; 126 (LOLE),
© Stephen Dalton/MP; 127 (UP), IrinaK/SS; 127 (LO), © Teguh Tirtaputra/DRMS; 128 (CTR), GUIDENOP/SS; 129 (UPRT), Steve Byland/SS; 129 (CTR LE), © Abeselom
Zerit/DRMS; 129 (CTR RT), © Drflash/DRMS; 129 (LO), © Smellme/DRMS; 130 (UP), © Arterra Picture Library/Alamy; 130 (CTR), © Jaymudaliar/DRMS; 130 (LO), ©
David Burke/DRMS; 131 (UP), © Robhainer/DRMS; 131 (CTR), © Steve Byland/DRMS; 131 (LO), Danny Alvarez/SS; 132 (UPRT), © Antti Siiskonen/DRMS; 132 (CTR LE), ©
Pavel Bořuta/DRMS; 132 (LORT), © Gerald Deboer/DRMS; 133 (UPLE), © Bluesunphoto/DRMS; 133 (UPRT), © Outdoorsman/DRMS; 133 (CTR), © Leerobin/DRMS; 134
(CTR), Michal Ninger/SS; 135 (CTR), © Auborddulac/DRMS; 136 (UPLE), john michael evan potter/SS; 136 (UPRT), Maggy Meyer/SS; 136 (LOLE), Chris Hill/SS; 136 (LORT),
encikAn/SS; 137 (UP), Filipe Frazao/SS; 137 (LO), HJ Weiermans/SS; 138–139 (CTR), © Steve Allen/DRMS; 138 (UPLE), © Norbert Buchholz/DRMS; 138 (CTR LE), Ivan
Kuzmin/SS; 138 (LO CTR RT), AS-kom/SS; 138 (LOLE), Shevs/SS; 138 (LORT), rorem/SS; 139 (UPLE), © Zhanghaobeibei/DRMS; 139 (UPRT), zimmytws/SS; 139 (UP CTR
RT), tatseN/SS; 139 (LO CTR RT), Tim Roberts Photography/SS; 139 (LOLE), © Ilja Ma ik/DRMS; 139 (LORT), Anton_Ivanov/SS; 141 (CTR), Franco Tempesta; 142 (UPLE), ©
Denis Doro/DRMS; 142 (UPRT), john michael evan potter/SS; 142 (LO), Maggy Meyer/SS; 143 (UP), © paul abbitt rml/Alamy; 143 (LOLE), © William Mahnken/DRMS; 143
(LORT), Nomad_Soul/SS; 144, © Alex Mustard/Nature Picture Library; 146 (UPLE), Dudarev Mikhail/SS; 146 (UPRT), Horse Crazy/SS; 146 (LOLE), Paul Nicklen/National
Geographic Creative; 146 (LORT), PHOTOCREO Michal Bednarek/SS; 147 (UPLE), © Gallinagomedia/DRMS; 147 (UPRT), outdoorsman/SS; 147 (CTR), Mika Heittola/SS;
147 (LO CTR), Julian W/SS; 147 (LORT), idiz/SS **Chapter 6:** 148 (CTR), © FLPA/Alamy; 150 (CTR), © Kerryn Parkinson/Caters News/ZUMAPRESS/Newscom; 152 (CTR), ©
Peter Scoones/Nature Picture Library; 153 (UP), © David Shale/Nature Picture Library; 153 (CTR), © Norbert Wu/MP; 153 (LO), © Mark Conlin/Alamy; 154 (UPRT), Joel
Sartore/NGC; 154 (LOLE), © Arco Images GmbH/Alamy; 155 (CTR), © Xunbin Pan/DRMS; 155 (LO), Tim Laman/NGC; 156 (CTR), Tadeu de Oliveira; 157 (UP), Dr Jodi
Rowley; 157 (CTR), Paul Marek; 157 (LO), Mark Gurney for Smithsonian/GI; 158 (UP), © Jurgen Freund/Nature Picture Library; 158 (CTR), © david tipling/Alamy; 158 (LO),
Dr K.P. Dinesh; 159 (UP), © Lynn M. Stone/Nature Picture Library; 159 (CTR), © Doug Allan/npl/MP; 159 (LO), © Jane Burton/Nature Picture Library; 160 (UP), © Dmytro
Pylypenko/DRMS; 160 (CTR), © Jesse Kraft/Alamy; 160 (LO), © Madeline Gray/The Palm Beach Post/ZUMAPRESS/Newscom; 161 (UP), © Rod Williams/Nature Picture
Library; 161 (CTR), © Lucy Pemoni/Reuters/Corbis; 161 (LO), © AP Photo/Kamran Jebreili; 162 (CTR), © Grant Glendinning/Alamy; 163 (UP), © Nurlan Kalchinov/Alamy;
163 (LO), Stuart Wilson/GI; 164 (UPLE), Norio Miyamoto/Naturwissenschaften; 164 (UPRT), © Daniel Heuclin/Nature Production/MP; 164 (LOLE), © FLPA/Alamy; 164
(LORT), © Piotr Naskrecki/MP; 165 (UPLE), © Nick Garbutt/Nature Picture Library; 165 (UPRT), © Eyal Bartov/Alamy; 165 (LOLE), William Stanley/The Field Museum;
165 (LORT), AP Photo/Gregory Guida/Durrell Wildlife Conservation Trust/PA Wire; 166–167 (CTR), © EPA-PHOTO/EPA/Nic Bothma/Newscom; 166 (UP), © Mark
MacEwen/Nature Picture Library; 166 (LO), © Juniors Bildarchiv GmbH/Alamy; 167 (UP), © David Shen/SeaPics.com; 167 (LO), © Franco Banfi/Nature Picture Library;
168 (LOLE), © The Natural History Museum/The Image Works; 168 (LORT), Robert Nicholls/Paleo Creations; 169 (UP), © Fortean/TopFoto/The Image Works; 169 (LO), ©
Jaime Chirinos/Science Source; 170 (UPLE), © Greg Harold/Auscape/MP; 170 (UPRT), Dr. Roland Hilgartner; 170 (LO), © Birdiegal717/DRMS; 171 (UP), ©
Hotshotsworldwide/DRMS; 171 (LOLE), © Barry Mansell/Nature Picture Library; 171 (LORT), © WaterFrame/Alamy; 172 (CTR), Frans Lanting/GI; 174 (UP), ©
blickwinkel/Alamy; 174 (LO), © Juniors Bildarchiv GmbH/Alamy; 175 (UP), © Tomatito26/DRMS; 175 (LO), © Ekaterina Pokrovsky/DRMS **Chapter 7:** 176 (CTR), ©
Peternile/DRMS; 178 (CTR), © Dykyostudio/DRMS; 180 (CTR), Auscape/UIG/GI; 181 (UP), © age fotostock Spain, S.L./Alamy; 181 (CTR), © Jxpfeer/DRMS; 181 (LO), ©
Mikhail Blajenov/DRMS; 182 (UP), © Photoshot Holdings Ltd/Alamy; 182 (LO), © Photowitch/DRMS; 183 (CTR), © Stefan Pircher/DRMS; 183 (LO), © Fred Bavendam/MP;
184 (CTR), © Barry Mansell/Naature Picture Library; 185 (RT1), © Richard Carey/DRMS; 185 (RT2), © Design Pics Inc./Alamy; 185 (RT3), © Todd Pusser/Nature Picture
Library; 185 (RT4), © Rademakerfotografie/DRMS; 185 (Rt5), bmse/GI; 186 (UP), © Johannes Gerhardus Swanepoel/DRMS; 186 (CTR), Donovan van Staden/SS; 186 (LO),
© Pär Edlund/DRMS; 187 (UP), altrendo travel/GI; 187 (CTR), © Bblood/DRMS; 187 (LO), Mark Newman/GI; 188–189 (CTR), © blickwinkel/Alamy; 188 (LE), © Jabruson/
Nature Picture Library; 188 (LO), © Jurgen Freund/Nature Picture Library; 189 (UP), © Daniel Heuclin/Nature Library; 189 (CTR), © All Canada Photos/Alamy; 189 (LO),
insaneDynamix (Darius Vakil)/GI; 190 (UP), paulrommer/SS; 190 (CTR), Eric Isselee/SS; 190 (LE), Dr. Morley Read/SS; 190 (RT), © Alex Hyde/Nature Picture Library; 191
(UPLE), aodaodaodaod/SS; 191 (UPRT), © Jurgen Freund/Nature Picture Library; 191 (CTR LE), © Andrew Mackay/Alamy; 191 (CTR RT), Willyam Bradberry/SS; 191
(LOLE), skynetphoto/SS; 191 (LORT), GondwanaGirl; 192 (UPLE), © Oriol Alamany/Nature Picture Library; 192 (UPRT), © 1000words/Dreamstim; 192 (LOLE), © Jonathan
Pledger/DRMS; 192 (LORT), © William Cortes/DRMS; 193 (UPLE), © Ingo Arndt/MP; 193 (UPRT), © Palko72/DRMS; 193 (LOLE), Mogens Trolle; 193 (LORT), Monika
Wieland/SS; 194–195 (CTR), olga_gl/SS; 194 (UP), Bonnie Taylor Barry/SS; 194 (LO), Sam DCruz/SS; 195 (UPLE), Sergey Uryadnikov/SS; 195 (UP CTR RT), Maggy Meyer/
SS; 195 (CTR LE), © Arco Images GmbH/Alamy; 195 (LORT), Erni/SS; 196 (UP), © Stocktrek Images, Inc./Alamy; 196 (LO), Franco Tempesta; 197 (CTR), Franco Tempesta;
198 (UPLE), © Pete Cairns/Nature Picture Library; 198 (UPRT), © Greg Balfour Evans/Alamy; 198 (LO), © Bob Jensen/Alamy; 199 (UP), © imageBROKER/Alamy; 199
(LOLE), © Nico Smit/DRMS; 199 (LORT), © ephotocorp/Alamy; 200 (CTR), Dennis W. Donohue; 201 (BACK), tulpahn/SS; 201 (LE), irin-k/SS; 201 (RT), wacpan/SS; 202
(UPRT), © Rolf Nussbaumer/Nature Picture Library; 202 (LOLE), © John Cancalosi/Alamy; 202 (LORT), © Brandon Cole Marine Photography/Alamy; 203 (UPRT), ©
Michael D. Kern/Nature Picture Library; 203 (CTR), © Frank Hecker/Alamy; 203 (LORT), © Luiz Claudio Marigo/Nature Picture Library; 204 (UP), © Sekarb | Dreamstime;
205 (LORT), © Woraphon Banchobdi | Dreamstime; 207, © Isselee/DRMS; 208, © Leerobin/DRMS

CREADITS

Copyright © 2015 National Geographic Society

All rights reserved. Reproduction of the whole or any part of the contents without written permission from the publisher is prohibited.

STAFF FOR THIS BOOK

Becky Baines, *Senior Editor*
Jen Agresta, *Project Editor*
Jim Hiscott, Jr., *Art Director*
Nicole Lazarus, *Designer*
Jay Sumner, *Photo Editor*
Paige Towler, *Editorial Assistant*
Sarah Wassner Flynn, *Writer*
Kathy Furgang, *Writer*
Jen Agresta, *Writer*
Sanjida Rashid and Rachel Kenny, *Design Production Assistants*
Colm McKeveny, *Rights Clearance Specialist*
Grace Hill, *Managing Editor*
Michael O'Connor, *Production Editor*
Lewis R. Bassford, *Production Manager*
Bobby Barr, Manager, *Production Services*
Susan Borke, *Legal and Business Affairs*

PUBLISHED BY THE NATIONAL GEOGRAPHIC SOCIETY

Gary E. Knell, *President and CEO*
John M. Fahey, *Chairman of the Board*
Melina Gerosa Bellows, *Chief Education Officer*
Declan Moore, *Chief Media Officer*
Hector Sierra, *Senior Vice President and General Manager, Book Division*

SENIOR MANAGEMENT TEAM, KIDS PUBLISHING AND MEDIA

Nancy Laties Feresten, *Senior Vice President*; Jennifer Emmett, *Vice President, Editorial Director, Kids Books*; Julie Vosburgh Agnone, *Vice President, Editorial Operations*; Rachel Buchholz, *Editor and Vice President, NG Kids magazine*; Michelle Sullivan, *Vice President, Kids Digital*; Eva Absher-Schantz, *Design Director*; Jay Sumner, *Photo Director*; Hannah August, *Marketing Director*; R. Gary Colbert, *Production Director*

DIGITAL

Anne McCormack, *Director*; Laura Goertzel, Sara Zeglin, *Producers*; Jed Winer, *Special Projects Assistant*; Emma Rigney, *Creative Producer*; Bianca Bowman, *Assistant Producer*; Natalie Jones, *Senior Product Manager*

The National Geographic Society is one of the world's largest nonprofit scientific and educational organizations. Founded in 1888 to "increase and diffuse geographic knowledge," the Society's mission is to inspire people to care about the planet. It reaches more than 400 million people worldwide each month through its official journal, *National Geographic,* and other magazines; National Geographic Channel; television documentaries; music; radio; films; books; DVDs; maps; exhibitions; live events; school publishing programs; interactive media; and merchandise. National Geographic has funded more than 10,000 scientific research, conservation, and exploration projects and supports an education program promoting geographic literacy.

For more information, please visit nationalgeographic.com, call 1-800-NGS LINE (647-5463), or write to the following address:
National Geographic Society
1145 17th Street N.W.
Washington, D.C. 20036-4688 U.S.A.

Visit us online at nationalgeographic.com/books

For librarians and teachers: ngchildrensbooks.org

More for kids from National Geographic: kids.nationalgeographic.com

For information about special discounts for bulk purchases, please contact National Geographic Books Special Sales: ngspecsales@ngs.org

For rights or permissions inquiries, please contact National Geographic Books Subsidiary Rights: ngbookrights@ngs.org

Paperback ISBN: 978-1-4263-1873-3
Reinforced library binding ISBN: 978-1-4263-1874-0

Printed in the United States of America
15/QGT-CML/1